Introduction

A person cannot know what opportunities God may present at any given time. Sometimes these appear to be highly unlikely. Dr. Young, Ken he insists me calling him, has given me such. I almost turned him down. Why would a man steeped in theology from a different ethnic cultural background ask a white, senior adult, middle school teacher to write an introduction for his book, especially given the reality that I have only known Ken for a few months? But herein lies one of his strengths.

I met Ken when he stepped outside his comfort zone and accepted a middle-school teaching position at the school I teach. A tough assignment it is, especially for one with little training for his job. I have watched him embrace the task, struggle with his classroom, and still love the students.

The quality that I have come to appreciate more than anything else about Ken is his communication with all people from all walks of life; and he interacts with them in such a Christ-like manner and spirit. He is so positive, uplifting, kind, and he interacts so well with people from a very broad range of walks, background, and ages. He is just a good man.

I genuinely believe Ken has something for all of us to read, meditate upon, ponder, learn, and strongly consider applying in our lives. As you read, think hard about what God may be trying to speak to you through Ken. I have already found such to be true for me.

Respectfully,

James Hill

Foreword

Many Christians desire to move beyond the box. What keeps many of us from doing so are the implications associated with such a move. It takes vision and courage to step outside of our comfort zone and experience the next dimension in God. This book is a practical guide that can motivate even the most timid believer and leader to move beyond a life of stagnation. God is next dimensional, and everything connected to Him must become.

Dr. Kenneth M. Young, Pastor of Restoration Millenia Church has poured himself out to the Body of Christ to encourage us toward the next dimension. This book that should be shared with every leader in your church who understands the need for radical and relevant ministry in the 21st century. It is written in a way that makes sense. The enemy's desire is that we remain sheltered in the boundary of the box and never explore beyond our comfort zone. Every person that God used to do great things always had to move from where they were to where He wanted them to be. God has always taken ordinary people and called them to extraordinary tasks. It really comes down to your willingness to be stretched, and your obedience to do what He asked you to do. I am encouraged that someone has taken on this difficult assignment and shared it with the body of Christ, so that each of us can live out what God intended for our lives.

I pray that you are blessed by this book, as I have been. I highly recommend it. This is a one-of-a-kind work that will transform your life as well as the life of your ministry. It is timely and necessary.

Bishop Joseph Warren Walker, 3,
Mt. Zion Baptist Church
Presiding Prelate,
FullGospel Baptist Church Fellowship

Can you handle it? God has opened the floodgates of heaven to release the supernatural. Can you handle what God is doing in your life? Can you handle being debt free? Can you handle being the head and not the tail? God has to take you through a process so you will be ready. He has to walk you through the process of lack so you can learn to trust Him for your finances. He has to walk you through sickness so you can learn to trust Him for your healing. The Bible says, **"*despise* not the day of small beginnings."** How you handle the small stuff will determine how you handle the big stuff. That's the principle of the kingdom "be faithful over a little, I will make you ruler of much." The final analysis is this. What it boils down to, is can you handle the overflow?

God has a plan to get you into position. Your position is paramount to the blessing. God releases certain blessings in certain places. You have to get into position in order to experience the overflow. You have been here before, but it was God who brought you back this time. In essence it is God who determines your next move. God gives you the promise then comes the problem to test the promise. If you can handle the test on this level God will give the provision for that level. "All of the promises of God are yes an amen."

You must allow God to prepare you for your purpose. I am going to discuss four levels that will allow you to walk into the next dimension. Your initial position is the ankle-deep level. Your next position is the knee-deep level, your third position is the waist deep level and your final level is the overflow. No matter what level you are on, *Going to the next dimension* will allow you to be in position so God can promote you and then you can move into the next dimension. Twenty-five years ago I was in Vicenza, Italy and God gave me a vision about the next dimension. It was deep water with buoys marking the levels of the river. Fear griped me because I thought, as the levels grew deeper I felt that I would be swept away, unable to navigate my way to safety. At the time I had no idea what God was doing. He was actually trying to guide me into a new experience with Him. All I knew was the traditional background and I felt overwhelmed. I am here to enlighten you that God wants your trust. Get ready to experience the next dimension!

CHAPTER ONE
PERMISSION TO GO TO THE NEXT DIMENSION
EZEKIEL 47: 1-3

1 Afterward, He brought me again unto the door of the house; and, behold, waters issued out from under the threshold of the house Eastward: for the forefront of the house stood toward the East, and the waters came down from under the right side of the house, at the South side of the alter.

2 Then he brought me out of the way of the gate northward, and led me about the way without unto the outer gate by the way that looked eastward; and, behold, there ran out waters on the right side.

3 And when the man that had the line in his hand went forth eastward, he measured a thousand cubits, and he brought me through the waters; the waters were to the ankles.

The door represents your opportunity. Opportunity means chance, or opening. God wants to extend a greater opportunity to because of you are open to what He wants to do in your life. When you are open to what God wants to do in you. It qualifies you for promotion of the next level. Promotion is what happens when preparation meets destiny. It's so important to be prepared. Preparation is to make or to get ready for something. Sometimes you have to go through a series of events to prepare for destiny. It has been said more than once "be ready when opportunity knocks."

You may find yourself at the ankle deep level. You may ask, what is the ankle deep level, or how do I know that I am on the ankle deep level. Good question, I'm glad you asked. He says the *water came up to his ankle*. Your ankles give support to your body. Your ankles represent the beginning. God must prepare you for your purpose. Ezekiel was brought to ankle-deep water. Ankle deep is like being in kindergarten. In kindergarten you don't change classes you stay in the same room all day so you won't get lost in the mix. Don't stop the process stay in kindergarten until God says you are ready for the next level. Your ankles are strong but they are also sensitive. For example, you can inadvertently step off a curve the wrong way, stumble and twist your ankle become crippled for life. God wants to prepare you so you don't become crippled. He wants you led into new experiences at deeper levels. Although you maybe strong you need God to show you the way.

4 Again he measured a thousand, and brought me through the waters; the waters were to the knees. Again he measured a thousand, and brought me through; the waters were to the loins.

5 Afterward he measured a thousand; and it was a river that I could not pass over; for the waters were risen, waters to swim in, a river that I could not be passed over.

Your preparation allows for God to bless you eminency. When you work with God, He will work with you. *"This time the water was up to my knees."* Your knees make it possible for you to run, walk, bend, and jump. Knee-deep water is like being in middle school. It is at this level that God can trust you with greater responsibility. See Matthew 25:14-30. You are right where God wants. Whatever you have is what you can handle. The bible says, "the blessings of the Lord makes one rich and adds no sorrow."

Middle school is tuff. It is imperative to follow the instructions of your teacher. There are five key things that must do to receive from God. (1) You must obey God even if it appears to go against reason. Your submission will determine whether you receive the blessing. (2) What God speaks it will require faith. "Trust in the Lord with all of thy hear and lean not unto your own understanding, but in all thy ways acknowledge and He shall direct thy paths." Proverbs 3:5, 6. (3) It will require real courage and willingness to do what He said. (4) What God says will line up with the Word of God. (5) When God speaks peace will be present. "O that thou hadst hearkened to my commandments! Then had thy peace been as a river, and thy righteousness as the waves of the sea." Isaiah 48:18. When you do what God tells you to do you will get there.

Your possibilities are imminent. Waist-deep is like being in high school you are not on your own, but the possibilities are imminent. You are half way there. Just like your waist is half way between your ribs and your hips. You are no longer depending on the stronger portion of your body to get you through tuff times you listening to God. "Not by power, nor might but by my spirit says the Lord. "Above all else, guard your heart, for it affects everything you do." Proverbs 4:23. "Humble yourself under the mighty hand of God that He may exalt you in due time." When you are in your season whatsoever you do will prosper because God has given permission for promotion.

Your dependence leads to productivity. *The river was too deep to cross without swimming* is like being in college. You are out of high school, but you are still a student in the educational system. What was impossible became possible through dependence upon God. God brought you through different levels so you could learn dependence and attain productivity. Ezekiel was as productive swimming in the deep as he was walking in the shadow waters because of his inability to act independently of God. Your inability to act independently of God increases your chances to succeed even against the greatest odds. See John 4:4. The water is symbolic of the Holy Spirit. The Holy Spirit will hold you up so you can be productive. It was predetermined for you to succeed you can't go under for going over. The overflow is the refreshing from the presence of the Lord that makes you perpetually productive. This is the time that Joel 3:18 and Revelation 22:1, 2 speak of. If you have not received what you are expecting hang on, its imminent! Stay on the line until He gets back to you. If you believe as I do, then it's worth the wait to receive your answer from the Lord. See Psalm 40:1-3. God wants to see if you can handle this before He gives you that.

CHAPTER TWO

YOU CAN'T SIT WHEN GOD WANT TO SHOW YOU SOMETHING

2 KINGS 7:3-7

3 And there were four leprous men at the entrance of the gate; and they said one to another. Why sit we here until we die?

4 If we say, We will enter into the city, then the famine is in the city, and we shall die there; and if we sit still here, we die also. Now, therefore, come, and let us fall unto the host of the Syrians; if they save us alive, we shall; and if they kill us, we shall but die.

5 And they rose up in the twilight, to go unto the camp of the Syrians; and when they were come to the edge of the camp of Syria, behold, there was no man there.

6 For the Lord had made the host of the Syrians hear a noise of chariots, and a noise of horses, even the noise of a great host; and they said one to another, Lo, the king of Israel hath hired against us the kings of the Hittites, and the kings of the Egyptians, to come upon us.

7 Wherefore, they rose and fled in the twilight, and left their tents, and theirs horses, and their asses, even the camp as it was, and fled for their life.

There will always be situations that are paradoxical to the promises of God. A paradox is a contradiction; you expect one thing and it turns out to be something different. You can't get bent out of shape and sit down because things don't work out.

There will always be situations that just don't add up and you are compelled to ask why? Have you ever ask yourself why do you do some of the stuff you do? Why you hook up with certain folks? Why do you try to impress people who really don't like you? Why do you smile when you really want to cry? Why would a Christian woman hook with an unsaved man, a thug, who is going no where? Why do people settle for less when they can have more? These are questions, which demand answers and things that make you go *"hummm."* We all have certain situations that paradoxical to the promises of God; situations that just don't add up and force us to ask why? How do you get around the whys? You can't sit when God got something to show you.

You gotta make a decision. Making a decision means accountability. Doesn't anybody want to be accountable? When you know better you will do better. Do you ever ask yourself why am I in the same position that I have been in for the last ten years? The leprous men asked, "why sit we here until we die?" Have you ever asked yourself why can't I step into the overflow of God-What's holding me back from experiencing God's best?

Why were lepers in the posture that they were in so long? Could it be that they were so frighten that they were at a stand still? Sometimes you can be so afraid that it brings you to a stand still. Do you know what fear is? Zig Ziglar says fear is false evident appearing real. Can we talk let us talk?

You've gotta change your posture. "And there were four leprous men at the entering in of the gate: and they said one to another, Why sit we here until we die? If we say, We will enter into the city, the famine is in the city, and we shall die there: and if we sit still here, we die also. Now therefore come, and let us fall unto the host of the Syrians: if they save us alive we shall live; and if they kill us, we shall but die." (2 Kings 7:3, 4).

Your posture means a whole lot with God. Your posture is your attitude about your situation. "He that come to God must believe that He is, and that he is a rewarder of them that diligently seek Him," Hebrews 11:6. You can miss your blessings if you are in the wrong posture. You can't be down when God wants you to be up.

The bottom line is you got to get up and get over it. You can't allow your circumstances to take control of you. Why sit in a posture pouting when God has promised you preferential treatment? Your posture means a whole lot with God. God is ready to bless you, but are you ready to be blessed?

They were in a posture of complacency, "And there were four leprous men at the entering in of the gate: and they said one to another, Why sit we here until we die?" If you are going to do anything positive you've gotta get up. Their current state was a rut. A rut is a grave with the walls knocked out.

If you would have asked them, "where are you going?" Their answer would be nowhere. You can't go nowhere if you are just sitting around. Some of us have been down too long, until everything is down. Our money is down, our health is down, and our attitude is down. The whole purpose for Jesus getting up is so you can get up; God does not want you to be down. If you are going to do anything you've gotta get up. Take off the grave clothes of complacency and get up.

If you take initiative you can move beyond your problems. God is waiting on you to change your posture. "And they rose up in the twilight, to go unto the camp of the Syrians: and when they were come to the uttermost part of the camp of Syria, behold, there was no man there." (2 Kings7: 5).

Nothing positive will happen until you make a change. "Faith is the substance of things hoped for and the evidence of things not seen," (Hebrews 11.1). If you want to see something positive happen in your life you've gotta put you faith into action. Even when you were saved you had to come "out of darkness into the marvelous light." You had to come up out of sin. "They rose up in the twilight." *Twilight.* What time of day is twilight? Twilight is early just before daybreak. It's not daylight, but it's not dark. It's a state of in between. What time did Jesus wake up, twilight? There is something about the early morning.

God wants to do something great in your life but there is something that is required of you. You've gotta make a change. It is said (insanity) is doing the same thing the same way and expecting different results. God sometimes creates a crisis to cure you of your complacency. God allowed that job fold so you could star your own business.

God knows how to take your troubles and turn them into triumphs. The lepers were in a do or die situation. If they did nothing they were going to die if they took the risk to do something they could die also. They made up their minds "even if kills me I'm going" to take the risk for something better.

When you change your posture God will make things Happen for you
 "For the Lord had made the host of the Syrians to hear a noise of chariots, and a nose of horses, even the noise of a

great host: and they said one to another; Lo, the king of Israel hath hired against us the kings of the Hittites, and the kings of the Egyptians, to come upon us. Wherefore they arose and fled in the twilight, and left their tents, and their horses, and their asses, even the camp as it was, and fled for their lives." (2 Kings 7: 6, 7).

When the lepers moved in the direction of their blessing God put their predators on the run. They changed their posture. When you change your posture you will be amazed of what God will do for you. When you move in the direction of your blessing God will make things happen for you. God wants to do something great in your life.

"The eyes of the Lord goes to and fro throughout the whole earth to show Himself strong on the behalf of those whose heart is loyal to Him." 2 Chronicles 16:9. God wants to do something great for you but you've gotta change your posture. You've gotta believe that God can turn it around.

He can give you greater victories in (valley) in the midst of impossibilities. God can do the impossible, but you've gotta have faith in Him to be able to do the extraordinary. Faith is a risk; you can't play it safe and please the Savior.

A lot of people get together but they don't believe their situation will change. What you need to do is to hook up with somebody who is willing to take a risk who believes that the Lord can do anything even the impossible. Like the church in the North Carolina when the pastor announced that we are going to pray for rain on Wednesday night because they had experienced a long drought. On Wednesday night, the church was packed. Some of the members looked and saw Sister Jones coming; she was wearing her rain hat, her raincoat, her galoshes and leaning on an umbrella. "Don't she know it's 99 degrees outside?" Somebody needs to go and tell the pastor.

Pastor look at Sister Jones. She must be crazy; she is wearing that rain hat, that raincoat, those goulashes and leaning on an umbrella. It is 99 degrees outside. She must

be crazy.

The Pastor asked her why she was dressed like that;

she told the pastor "I've come to pray for rain. I believe

that when we pray, we better believe that God will answer

prayer. I'm in it to win it. I'm coming in faith, I believe

God is going to turn things around.

That's what the lepers did they changed their

posture and God made things positive things happen for

them. Yall this what I'm trying to say you don't need to sit

in complacency any longer. It's time to make a change and

see what God has in store for us in 2004. God is ready to

heal but you are wondering what are the people are going

to say. God has been telling you to praise Him more but

you are wondering what are the people are going to say.

When you change your posture God will make things

happen for you.

CHAPTER THREE

CONFRONTING THE INTIMDATOR

1 SAMUEL 24:11-15

11 Moreover, my father, see, yea, see the skirt of thy robe in my hand; for in that I cut off the skirt of thy robe, and killed thee not, know thou and see that there is neither evil nor transgression in mine hand, and I have not sinned against thee; yet thou huntest my soul to take it.

12 The Lord judge between me and thee, and the Lord avenge me of thee; but mine hand shall not be upon thee.

13 As saith the proverb of the ancients, Wickedness proceedeth from the wicked; but mine hand shall not be upon thee.

14 After whom is the king of Israel come out? After whom dost thou pursue? After a dead dog! After a flea!

15 The Lord, therefore, be judge, and judge between me and thee, and see, and plead my cause, and deliver me out of thine hand.

All of us have some haters. You can't allow your haters to stop you from reaching y our destiny. Until you confront what you are afraid of you will forever be on the run. The intimidator wants to control you and to stop you from reaching your destiny. Satan wants to spoil your success. He uses people and natural occurrences to try and frustrate you spiritually. He is trying to get your focus off of God and on him. Fear is the tactic of the intimidator to try to stop you, but you have to remind your intimidator that God has anointed me to prosper ain't nothing he can do about. Intimidation is to make timid; frighten or to control by fear. The intimidator seeks to control you thorough the fear of rejection, fear of failure, a fear of success, a fear of responsibility, a fear of loneliness, even a fear of fear itself. Don't let spiritual attacks hold you back any longer "God prepares a table before me in the presence of my enemies" You gotta stop letting the devil chase you and start chasing the devil. You need to start fighting fear with focus. The best defense against fear is never to take your eyes off of Jesus. "No weapon formed against me shall prosper."

Call him out (v.11). "Moreover, my father, see, yea, see the skirt of thy robe in my hand: for in that I cut off the skirt of thy robe, and killed thee not know thou and see that there is neither evil nor transgression in mine hand, and I have not sinned against thee; yet thou huntest my soul to take it."

David is saying to Saul the intimidator I could have killed you, but that's not my destiny. "I will not touch God's anointed." My destiny is to be the anointed king of Israel. In God's timing I will have your seat. You must confront the intimidator in order to conquer the intimidator. You deal with the situation or it will. Deal with you.

Call it what it is (v.13) "As saith the proverb of the ancients, wickedness proceedeth from the wicked: but mine hand shall not be upon thee." Call it like you see it. Sometimes the enemy you are fighting is the devil in you. Saul was trying to kill David but the real devil was not David but it was Saul. It was the enemy "inner me." You cab be you own worst enemy. Jealous is resentful of another's success. Saul became jealous of David when he killed Goliath. The people started singing a song Saul killed a thousand, David killed ten thousand. Jealous a sin that will grow into hatred which can led to murder. The devil hates Christians because we took his place as the praise and worship leader. When God fired Lucifer God gave us the job to praise Him. God gave David Saul' job because Saul disobeyed God commands to destroy the Amalekites. Don't you think you can make your intimidator like you he wants to kill you? You gotta call what it is. Terror from the intimidator he wants to distract, deny, and destroy.

It's time to put the brakes on (vv.14, 15). "After whom is the king of Israel come out? After whom dost thou pursue? After a dead dog, after a flea? The Lord therefore be judge, and judge between me and thee, and see,
and plead my cause, and deliver me out of thine hand."

I believe that you must develop the habit of constantly taking inventory, which will lead to knowing when to say "when." You'll learn when to put the brakes so that you don't crash and know when to keep going so that you stay on the road. Saul was about to crash and David wanted to stay on the road to destiny. David made of his mind to confront Saul. David decided it was time to put the brakes on. You are the King of Israel why have you come after me?

As saints, you have been anointed with "fresh oil" it's time to put the brakes on and confront the intimidator. You've gotta make up your mind I will not be control by this intimidator any longer I'm in covenant. "He has anointed me with "fresh oil" my head has been anointed with oil and my cup runs over." To anoint is to invest with power. God has given you the power to cast out devils, power to lay hands on the sick and they shall recover; power to tread on serpents and scorpions, power over the enemy and power to speak with new tongues, why are you afraid when you have so much power? (Mark 16:17,18/ Luke 10: 19). Why are you intimidated when God has given you the power to put the brakes on?

The intimidator can't stop you because God has anointed you He is the one who prepares a table before you in the presence of your intimidator. Don't let spiritual attacks hold you back any longer you have power to defeat the enemy. Now is your time to walk in your purpose. Now is your time to fulfil your ministry assignment. Now is your time for you to be the head and not the tail. Now is your time for you to be above and not beneath. Now is your time for you to stop running from the devil, its time for the devil to run from you! You will reach your destiny. Saul had his time now it was David's time to be King.

CHAPTER FOUR

IT'S YOUR MOMENT TO MAKE YOUR MOVE

JOSHUA 3:1-4

It's late but its not too late to step into the blessings of God. Even if you are behind schedule don't delay, get a move on, breakthrough is on its way. It's critical for you to move now "timing is everything". If you want what God has for you, you gotta make an effort to move toward it. Your window of opportunity is limited by time it will not remain open. A _moment_ is a short space in time; therefore it's critical for you to make your move now. It's your moment to be blessed of God its up to you to walk into what God has prepared for you. Many times people miss their blessings because they are not ready for them. God is ready to bless you He is ready to turn things around for you, now it's up to you to go after it. It's your moment to make your move.

You need the spirit of discernment so you can sense what God has in store for your life. "And they commanded the people, saying, when ye see the Ark of the Covenant of the Lord your God."

God wants to do something great in your life. The saint who operates in discernment will be able to "pick up" on the subtle movement of God in and around them.

"The eyes of the Lord goes to and fro throughout the whole earth to show Himself strong on the behalf of those whose heart is loyal to Him." 2 Chronicles 16:9. God wants to do something for you and you've got to be ready for it. If you are ahead of Him you will miss Him, if you are behind Him He will pass you by. You gotta get a move on because God wants to show you something.

Great EXPECTATION – God has revealed to me that He is going to release blessings on those who expect them. The year of 2004 will be the year of double increase for those who will stick with the plan of God.
and the paradox of our faith has to be expecting the unexpected. We will not just pray for rain, but we will pray while holding umbrellas.

You've get up get a move on because God wants to show you something.
If you want to get to the place of your blessing you gotta stick with God's plan for your life. "And the priest the Levites bearing it"

God's plan for the people was to follow the priests. The way to get to the place of your blessing is your willingness to stick with God's plan for your life.

Uncompromised OBEDIENCE – the one who operates within a responsible relationship with God will obey God. In order to walk into your place of blessing, to win in your finances and win in your family you must obey God. If you want to capture your moment you must develop a spirit of uncompromised obedience. Obedience is better than sacrifice. Obedience is moving when the Lord says so. Obedience is going forth based upon the spoken or revealed word of God in your life.

"Obey them that have rule over you, and submit yourselves: for they watch for your souls as they that must give account that they may do it with joy, and not with grief: for that is unprofitable for you." Hebrews 13:17.

"If ye be willing and obedient, ye shall eat the good of the land," Isaiah 1:19. If you want to be blessed you gotta stick to the plan of God. The year of 2004 will be the year of double increase for those who will stick with the plan of God.

If you don't make your move you will miss your moment. "Then ye shall remove from your place and go after it." This is your season of double increase; however, in order to experience double you must be a person of obedience. "Then ye shall remove from your place and go after it." Your obedience will cause you to "prosper in due season."

It takes faith to obey God. Your moment is waiting on you but it's up to you to make your move. In order to move into your season of winning in your finances and winning in your family you must walk in faith. All things are possible to them that believe.

No matter how long you have been down you gotta have faith to move; it's your moment. It's never too late to make your move. Your future is great therefore you must not let your past rob you of your future. God had great things in store for Israel; it was their moment. They had to make their move now you have to make yours.

Mark tells us of a woman who had been sick for twelve years [4,380 days; 625.7 weeks; 52.1 months] but she did not she miss her moment she got her healing. She made up her mind to stop living with the minuses and moved on to better heath. She made up her mind that things were going to get better Jesus is in town.

You gotta believe when Jesus shows up things are going to get better!

When opportunity knocks you gotta answer the door. The Mosaic Law was a blessing blocker but she took her chance to see Jesus.
No matter what you have gone through things can change. No matter how broke you have been things can change. No matter how sick you have been things can change. No matter what the cost things can change, make your move?

The results of timing. According to John Maxwell, timing is everything.
Wrong action wrong time equals disaster

Right action wrong time equals resistance

Wrong action right time is a mistake

Right action right time equals success

It was the right action at the right time for Ester. It was time for her to make her move. It's time for you to make your move your season is waiting on you. It's up to you to walk into it. It has been stated that "timing is everything".

Understanding this makes for a great journey with God. For when we talk about our season we are really talking about timing. In Psalm 1:3, it stated that the one who operates within a responsible relationship with God will "prosper in due season." Your recognition that God's system of operating is governed by "due season" will go a long way in determining the extent of God's anointing in your life. Ecclesiastes 3:1 declares that "there is a time for everything and a season for every activity under the Heaven." How then do we capture our season? Let me suggest the following:

Desire the spirit of discernment. V.1 "Blesses is the man who walks not in the counsel of the ungodly, nor stands in the path of sinners, nor sits in the seat of the scornful." Discernment is simply understanding the mind of God and clearly hearing the Eternal's voice about your situation. The saint who operates in discernment will be able to move at the right time. You will "pick up" on the subtle movement of God in and around you.

Develop the spirit of uncompromising obedience. V.2"But his delight is in the law of the Lord; and in his law doth he meditate day and night." Obedience is moving when the Lord says so. It is going forth based upon the spoken or revealed word of God in your life. It is declaring all other forces non-issues when it comes to the Word of the Lord. You move despite how it looks and what others perceive and pronounce. The key to this is an unwavering commitment to the Word of God in your life.

You gotta declare your destiny. V.3 "And he shall be like a tree planted by the rivers of water, that bringeth forth his fruit in his season; his leaf also shall not wither;

and whatsoever he doeth shall prosper. If you declare or decree a thing it shall be established, Job 22:28. This is one of the more meaningful passages in the biblical record. To understand the power of what you declare and decree is one of the most liberating principles. I am what I choose to consistently call myself and my destiny is tied to my identity. If I declare life, through my declaration I give birth to life. What are you declaring?

Develop the discipline and devotion of sowing seeds. I must report that far too many of us see sowing seeds as a manipulative tool extracting monies from saints. However, I have learned that any practice that is biblical that I adopt works for me even if others misappropriate it.

Sowing seeds or giving sacrificial positions me to receive from the Lord in a way that nothing else can. In 2 Corthiains 9, Paul challenges the Body of Christ to avail themselves to giving that is both a ministry and a blessing. Any saint willing to give at that level will receive abundantly. What are you doing with your seeds? That is the key question.

CHAPTER FIVE
DON'T SIT ON YOUR OPPORTUNITY

Mark 5:25-29

God has given you great potential you've gotta put it to work for you. God has given you great potential to think you've gotta put your mind to work for you. Don't sit on it. If your mind can conceive it you can achieve it. God has given you the ability to get things done. You can't afford to sit on it you've gotta get busy. You can do whatever you say you can do. God has given you great potential to speak you can't afford to sit on it, you've gotta open your mouth and speak up. It's your moment to make your move you can't afford to sit on it this opportunity.

Death and life are in the power of the tongue. It's late but its not too late to step into the blessings of God. Even if you are behind schedule get a move on breakthrough is on its way. It takes faith to receive what God has for you. If what you are believing God for does not require faith then you are not pleasing God.

If you want the blessing of God you've gotta believe God will make great things happen for you. Don't sit on your faith, faith is your key to you receiving the promises of God and seeing them coming alive in your life.

The woman of our text made a decision to do something about her situation. This woman needed healing.

What do you need from God? It's your time to get your blessings.

Don't let your past rob you of your future –(v.25) "And a certain woman, which had an issue of blood twelve years." Your future is great you can't afford to let your past rob you of your future. Psalms 118:23 say, "this is the day that the Lord, hast made, I will rejoice and be glad in it."

God is more concerned about your future than He is about your past. He has no memory of your past. You gotta let your past go so you can experience what God has for you now. Don't sit on it.

You've gotta release your past so you can reach for your future. You are your worst nightmare. Things will get better when you forgive yourself of your past failures that God has forgotten about. Don't sit on past failures move into your future.

What's holding you back that you need to let go of so you can move on? What issues haven't you dealt with that have kept you from going to the next level?

Stop living with minuses – (v.26) "And had suffered many things of many physicians, and had spent all that she had, and was nothing bettered, but rather grew worse"

This woman knew misery beyond measure. "And had suffered many things of many physicians." Her doctors left her penniless and filled with pain. When you put your trust in man you will be left penniless and filled with pain.

She was determined to stop living with minuses. For twelve years she had lived without comfort and consideration of others because she was sick.
She was determined to stop living with minuses.

What pain have you been carrying around for years?

Some of us have been carrying excess baggage for at least twelve years or more. What pain or problems that you have been carrying around for years that you need to get rid of?

When you look at the airline it has limits of how much baggage you are allowed to carry when you abroad the plane. They know that it is unsafe to carry excess baggage when you travel. How much excess baggage are you carrying today?

Today you need to make the decision to stop with minuses…Get rid of the excess baggage…The hymn say, Oh what needless pain we bare all because we do not carry everything to God in prayer.

Sisters don't sit on it. Get rid of that old baggage.

It's time to make your move – (vv.27-29) "When she had heard of Jesus, came in the press behind, and touched his garment. For she said, If I may touch but his clothes, I shall be well. And straightway the fountain of her blood was dried up; and she felt in her body that she was healed of that plague"

When opportunity knocks, don't sit on it, you've gotta answer the door. According to the Mosaic Law she was not allowed to come near the priest or the temple. The Mosaic Law was a blessing blocker but, she didn't sit on her opportunity she took her chance to see Jesus.

No matter what you have to go through to get your blessings, don't sit on it. No matter how broke you have been don't sit on it, "God will supply all your needs according to His riches in glory." No matter how sick you have been don't sit on it, "by His stripes you were healed." No matter what the cost don't sit on it, "God will make a way out of no way."

Make your move? Don't sit on it.
No matter what you have to go through, no matter what risk God will reward you. When you trust God things will change.

Story…

CHAPTER SIX

STAY 'IN THE FLOW

GENESIS 26:15-18

The greatest hindrance to the present move of God is the past move of God. The key to your success in ministry is to be sensitive to the spirit and to stay in the flow. 2005 is the year of overflow. If you want to be a part of the overflow; you've gotta stay in the flow of the Holy Spirit so you can reap the blessings of God. You can't afford to get out of the flow of the spirit of God and allow what God has promised you to slip through the cracks.

Isaac stayed in the flow of his daddy. He had to dig again the wells that his daddy had dug because the enemy covered them up. It is our responsibility to stay in the flow of the Holy Spirit so we can enjoy victory in ministry. We are digging by the dictates of the Holy Spirit. We are digging where our fathers have dug. When you put trust in the Lord he will direct your path.

Your destiny is tried to staying in the flow of GOD.

If you want to go to the next level You've gotta stay connected- (v.15)

"For all the wells which his father's servants had digged in the days of Abraham his father, the Philistines had stopped them, and filled them with earth."

Isaac was connected to the vision of his daddy. Abraham was Isaac's daddy he was connected to a great man. He found the place where his daddy had dug wells and he started digging. You've gotta stay connected to the vision of your father if you want to defeat the enemy. When you get in place you will flow into your purpose and prosperity will follow. When you are connected with the vision of your heavenly father you will prosper. "I will bless you coming in and bless you going out…" (Deuteronomy 28:1)

Life will let you know when it's time to make a change- (vv.16&17).
"And Abimelech said unto Isaac, Go from us; for thou art much mightier than we. And Isaac departed from there, and pitched his tent in the valley of Gerar, and dwelt there." We hate change, but change is everywhere. Isaac made a change because it was time for it.

Life dictates making a change. It will come whether you want it or not. The key to successful ministry is to be sensitive to the Holy Spirit and to make a change when He leads you too. If you miss the move of God you will miss your destiny. If you follow the crowd you will get lost you get lost in the crowd. Every ten years there will be a major change in your ministry, marriage, and how you manager your life.

The worst kind of ministry, marriage or management is to have is one stuck in the wilderness of complacency. This Church is going to operate in the fullness of the Holy Spirit we are not going to get stuck in the wilderness of complacency. Carnal people cannot see the need the change they want to see things remain the same. "And Abimelech said unto Isaac, Go from us; for thou art much mightier than we. Your enemy can bless you by pushing into your destiny.

Abimelech wanted Isaac to relocate. "And Isaac departed from there, and pitched his tent in the valley of

Gerar, and dwelt there." Isaac's move to Gerar and he was blessed. If God leads you to it He will lead you through it. Life can push you into your destiny. Sickness can push you into your healing. Debt can push you into financial freedom. Divorce can push you into a successful relationship.

The push for change is about the kingdom. Fear is to be afraid of change because fear doesn't want you to grow. Fear knows when you are flowing with God you will grow.

"Planted by the rivers of water, that bringeth forth its fruit in its season." (Psalm 1:3). God has not given us the spirit of fear, but of power, love and a sound mind." (2 Timothy 1:7). Fear makes you do irrational stuff, but God has given us a sound mind.

When you stay in the flow of leadership your haters can't stop you- (v.18)
"And Isaac digged again the wells of water, which they had digged in the days of Abraham, his father; for the Philistines had stopped them after the death of Abraham:

and he called their names after the names by which his father had called them."

Your haters can't stop what God has started, that's why it's the devil hate true leaders. It's important to stay in the flow of leadership because they represent God among the people. "And Isaac digged again the wells of water, which they had digged in the days of Abraham, his father; for the Philistines had stopped them after the death of Abraham."

Abraham was called the friend of God. He taught his son how to hear God's voice. You gotta know whose voice you are following. Jesus said, "my sheep know my voice for they follow me. But a stranger will they not follow, but will flee from him; for they know not the voice of strangers." (John 10:4&5).

How can I know the true voice from a false voice? The Holy Spirit you will bear witness with your spirit its up to you who you will follow. When you follow the true voice you will prosper.

"And he shall be like a tree planted by the rivers of water, that bringeth forth its fruit in its season;" (Psalm 1:3). When you stay in the flow of leadership your haters can't stop you. "No weapon that is formed against you shall prosper."

Stay in the flow. When people throw dirt into the wells Isaac started the process of digging again. You can't let people stop you. You've gotta shake it off and put it under your feet. The people who were with Isaac were blessed because they followed Isaac's leadership. Because they stayed in the flow he led them to where the water were flowing. If you are wondering when God is going to open up the widows of heaven God is waiting on you to get in the flow. Once you get in His will stay out of His way.

If you want to be blessed you've gotta stay connected with the leader God has appointed over you. When you get in the flow…"It is like the precious ointment upon the head, that ran down upon the bread, even Aaron's bread; that went down to the skirts of his garments." (Psalm 133:2).

The <u>anointing</u> to prosper will be released into & upon your life because you stayed in the flow. There are some people who won't be blessed because won't flow with leadership can't nobody tell them nothing. There are problems that you can't solve by yourself you need a man of God to speak into your life. Amos 3:7 "Surely the Lord God will do nothing, but the revealeth his secrets unto his servants, the prophets."

You can't get what you need for the psyche hotline, a hireling. A hireling is a preacher who does what the people tell him afraid that they will cut his check. You've gotta be in the flow of leadership if you want to get something from God. "Where there is no vision the people perish," (Proverbs 29:18).

CHAPTER SEVEN

IT'S TIME FOR THAT WALL TO COME DOWN

JOSHUA 6:1-5

In 2003, the Orlando Magic basketball team has lost seven games strait. Coach Doc Rivers was interviewed and the reporter asked him how he feels he told the reporter it feel like I have run up against a wall. All of us have walls. Walls of debt, walls of disobedient children, walls of trouble on your job, walls of poor health, walls of misunderstanding and there are walls of disappointment. A wall is an upright structure that prevents the passage from one side to the other.

What kind of wall do you have that need to fall? I'm on assignment to tell you what you need to do to get your wall to fall! Can we talk? Let us talk. God made a promise with Abraham to give him a land flowing with milk and honey. God wanted to make good on His promise to give them the land, but there was a wall standing between what God had promised and what they could claim as their possession. The good news of this text is your wall can come down. God has a strategy to get your wall to fall.

The walls of Jericho were gigantic they were 25 feet high and 20 feet wide. It does not matter how gigantic your wall is it will fall. Don't allow your walls to intimidate you, God is going to bring them down.

What do I need to do to get my wall to fall?

You gotta let the Lord help you to see your way clear – (v.2)

"And the Lord said unto Joshua, See, I have given into thine hand Jericho, and the king thereof, and the mighty men of valor."

God will give you the victory but you gotta let Him help you to see your way clear. Faith is the substance of things

hoped for and evidence of things not seen. Hebrews 11:1
We walk by faith and not by sight. 2Cornthian 5:7
If you are sick need to let the Lord show you your healing.
He was wounded for our transgression He was bruised for
our iniquities: the chastisement for our peace was upon
Him; and with his stripes we are healed. Isaiah 53:4.

If you are experiencing financial trouble let the Lord
show you His blessings. Bring ye all the tithes into the
storehouse, that there may be meat in mine house, and
prove me now herewith, saith the Lord of hosts, if I will
not open you the windows of heaven, and pour you out a
blessing, that there shall not be room enough to receive it.
Malachi 3:10.

If you seem to not be able to get it together let the
Lord show you who you are. You are blessed coming in
and blessed going out, you are the lender and not the
borrower, you are the head and not the tail, you are above
and not beneath. Deuteronomy 28:6,12,13.

You gotta stick with the plan that God has given you – (vv.3, 4)

And ye shall compass the city, all ye men of war, and go around about the city once. Thus shalt thou do six days. And seven priests shall bear before the ark seven trumpets of rams' horn: and the seventh day ye shall compass the city seven times, and the priest shall blow with the trumpets.

Praise is God' s way to conquer a city. Your obedience to stick with God's plan for your life will release blessings. If you want to be blessed you had better do what God told you to do. God told Joshua what to do and he did it. Joshua was successful because he did what God told him to do. Have not I commanded thee? Be strong and of a good courage; be not afraid, neither be thou dismayed: for the Lord the God is with thee whithersoever thou goest. Joshua 1:9.

You have fear because of what somebody might say. Somebody in here God has told to start praising Him more but you are afraid of what the people might say about you. You are afraid that they might not like you anymore.

"And ye shall compass the city, all ye men of war, and go around about the city once. He gave specific instructions on how to gain victory over the city of Jericho. God is telling us how to gain the victory over our problems. (1) The pattern, (2) the priest, (3) the people, and (3) then the praise. Thus shalt thou do six days. The pattern days. And seven priest the priest shall bear before the ark seven trumpets of rams' horns: and the seventh day ye the people shall compass the city seven times, and the priests shall blow with the trumpets." the praise breakthrough comes through your praise.

Trumpets were used in military battles. The sounding of the trumpets was a call to arms. The Horn in Hebrew. Your (shoh-far) means to lift one's voice to utter the words of instructions of God. God has given us instructions to praise Him. Praise ye the Lord. Praise Him in the dance; Praise Him on the high sounding cymbal. Let everything that has breath praise the Lord. "Let the high praises of God be in their mouth, and a two-edged sword in their hand," (Psalm 149:6) Praise is a warfare strategy.

If you want victory you gotta start shouting for it – (v.5)

"And it shall come to pass, that when they make a long blast with the ram's horn, and when ye hear the sound of the trumpet, all the people shall shout with a great shout; and the wall of the city shall fall down flat, and the people shall ascend up every man straight before him."

There is <u>victory</u> in your shout. There is always something to shout about. There are some many unfortunate things happening, somebody just had an accident, somebody just died and somebody had a heart attack. When these bad things haven't happen to you, you have something to shout about. God gave them the victory because they shouted. God will give you victory over your circumstances if you shout. If you want to see something you gotta say something.

There is power in praise. The key to your survival is praise.

Praise is your weapon of warfare. Your praise is your proof of what God can do. Not only is praising your proof of what God can do, but of what He will do. They praised Him before the wall fell. God brought their wall down, and He is going to your wall down. He can turn it things around if you just praise Him.

Now I know why shouting John had to shout. There was a man name shouting John. John loved to praise the Lord. God had been good to him and he was not ashamed to get his praise on. Shouting John joined this church that was a dead church. They didn't believe in saying amen and hallelujah. They believed that you should have certain decorum in church.

Shouting John didn't feel that way. Every Sunday he would praise the Lord. They called a meeting and said let's go have a talk with shouting John. They decided to give him a visit. They saw him on his field he was plowing a field with his mule. They walked over to him and said John we have had a meeting we have decided that you make too much noise praising God in church.

You praise so loud we can hardly hear we came to tell you to stop praising so loud, if you don't we are going to have to ask you to leave the church.

John looked at the church people and said, "you see all this land you've standing on? God gave it to me. You see all of my cattle? God gave it to me. You see my healthy arms and legs to plow this field? God gave it to me. If you feel that you gotta put me out, go right ahead because I can't stop praising God. If you put me out of the church, Ill praise Him right out here on the land He gave me. I just gotta praise Him. I just can't keep it to myself. If you got a wall that need to fall you better get your praise on? Your

Shout will cause your wall to fall.

CHAPTER EIGHT
LEAVE THE PAST BEHIND YOU
PHILLIPPIANS 3:13-14

God is more concerned about your future than He is about your past. He has no memory of your past. "He has cast it into the sea of forgetfulness to remember them no more." We are our own worst nightmare. Things that we remember about our past and ourselves God has forgotten. Anything the devil had in mind of doing to us it would be less than the pain we would inflict upon ourselves.

The devil would not have much to do if God would leave us to ourselves because we would do the greater damage. If God would leave us to ourselves we would self-destruct. We've gotta learn how to forgive ourselves before we can reach for our futures. The Bible says, "Satan comes before God day and night to accuse us. And they overcame him by the blood of the Lamb, and the by the word of their testimony," (Revelation 12:11).

Paul had to bring his own mind under subjection before he could remind others about his future. Paul was more concerned about his restoration than his resume because his restoration pointed to where he was going and his resume was where he had been. When people remind you of your past remind them of your future.

Your future is too great to allow your past to stop you- (V.13). "Brethren, I count not myself to have apprehended: but this one thing I do, forgetting those things which are behind"

Before you can remind people about your future you've gotta forgive yourself. God is more concerned about your future than He is about your past. He has no memory of your past.

Paul had to bring his own mind under subjection before he could remind others about his future. God's know how to sweeten up a bitter situation. Paul's defense before Agrippa: I use to persecute the Church now I'm preaching at the Church. "At midday, O king, I saw in the way a light from heaven, above the brightness of the sun, shining round about me"…since that day I started preaching, (Acts 26:13).

You've gotta come correct before you can remind others about your future. You've gotta convince yourself first. The number one problem you, you've gotta be convinced first. That's like you saying that you've been called to preach but you are not convinced that you have been called to preach. You've gotta be convinced first, before you can convince others. It is virtuously impossible to convince others if you are not convinced!

You've gotta release your past so you can reach for your future -(V.13, b).
" Reaching forth unto those things which are before." Forgiveness is release. You've gotta forgive yourself first. Once you have forgiven yourself you can reach for your future.

Prayer of serenity "God grant me the serenity to accept the things that I cannot change, the courage to change the things that I can and the wisdom to know the difference."

God has great things in store for you. You can't allow your past to rob you of your future. You need the spirit of discernment so you won't get stuck in the past. God has great things in store for you, you've gotta move on. Paul did not know what was in store but he could sense that something better was up ahead.

Don't let drama stop you There is a blessing in pressing - (V.14). "I press toward the mark for the prize of the high calling of God in Christ Jesus."

You can't let drama stop you there is a blessing in pressing. Press means to demand on you. When you demand of yourself you will move toward your future. When you move toward your future your relationship with Jesus becomes tight. God says, "I know the thoughts that I think towards you, saith the Lord, thoughts of peace, and not of evil, to give you and an expected end," (Jeremiah

29:11). You've gotta forgive yourself so you can enjoy your future. Your future is filled with wonderful things. "If ye be Christ's, then are ye Abraham's seed and heirs according to the promise," (Galatians 3:29).

Your relationship with Jesus is like a card game. Jesus is the dealer. He is ready to deal you a good hand, but you've gotta come to the table so you can be in the game. You can expect to receive a winning hand when Jesus is dealing the cards. He may throw you an Ace Spade, a King Spade, or a 2/Diamond.

He will not throw you a joker. A joker is a prankster card. Jesus is for real. When He says, "you are head and not the tail; above and beneath; He is for real. The lender and not the borrower; blessed coming in and blessed going out. He is not a prankster…"We are more than conquerors through Him that loved us," (Romans 8:37).

There is a blessing in pressing.

CHAPTER NINE

CLIMB HIGER

LUKE 19:1-5

Revelation to see God for who He is requires effort.

What is revelation? Revelation means God has given you

the answer to what was a secret to you. You've gotta make a decision to move up if you want to see what you never seen before. That's why it's necessary to climb up above the crowd.

You need the Lord. (v.1). "Then Jesus entered and passed through Jericho." It appears that Zacchaeus had it all together, but looks can be deceiving. It appears that he was in place but in all actually he was out of place. It's important for you to be in place. God is a God of timing.

Like a timing pattern in football. The quarterback is throwing the ball to a particular spot. It is the job of the receiver to get there and receive the ball. The receiver will encounter opposition. It is the job of the defense to stop forward progress. If the opposition can stop your forward progress you will lose the game. What keeps the offense from throwing in the towel?

They see a goal. That why you need a vision. "Where there is no vision the people perish." Proverbs 29:18. Habakkuk 2:2 says "write the vision and make it plan that they who read the vision may run." What keeps you in the game despite opposition? Zacchaeus was out of place and was about to lose the game until Jesus showed up. He was in Jericho. Everything that we know about Jericho is not good. Jericho was the city that Joshua cursed. Jericho was the city where a man fell among thieves. Although Jericho had a bad rap, Jesus was on His way to reach those who were looking to <u>climb above the crowd.</u>

Sometimes stuff can get between you and the Lord. (V.2, 3). "Now behold, there was a man named Zacchaeus who was a chief tax collector, and he was rich. And he sought to see who Jesus was, but could not because of the crowd, for he was of short statue." Sometimes your blessing can get between you and the Lord. He was a tax collector and he was rich. He thought that his wealth could satisfy his thirst.

Although he was wealthy he came up short. Zacchaeus was a little man who was at war with himself. He was Jewish working for a Roman government, but he ran ahead. Sometimes your condition ought to make you run ahead. The moment you understand who you are you will run ahead. "And he sought to see who Jesus was, but could not because of the crowd, for he was of short statue." His littleness demanded he do something. When we put God in a box, our littleness demands that we do something. If you want to do better you can't sit, you've gotta run ahead.

The day that you discover that your issues are blocking your ability to see the Lord it's time to put some space between you and your issues. The secret is not to repeat the same mistake. Low self-esteem makes you depend on people when you need the Lord. If you need people to validate you, you ain't spiritual. If don't run ahead the crowd will block what God wants to do for you. When you run ahead, you've gotta do the next thing.

Climb above the crowd. (v.4). To climb is to elevate your mind set above the crowd. "So he ran ahead and climbed up into a sycamore tree to see Him, for He was going to pass that way." Sycamore tree has high limbs and slippery bark. It hard work to climb above the crowd.

It's hard work to think differently, to overcome your fears and to grow up. God can't work with you when Ray-Ray and pookey control the way you think. God, give me wisdom to seek after you. "When a mans ways please the Lord, He makes even his enemies to be at peace with him." Proverbs 16:7.

God is going to show you some stuff when you elevate your thinking. "I am what I am because of God." I am where I am because I had to think bigger. I had to elevate my praise…I had to do what God told me to do. God is orchestrating things so I had to climb. My littleness was a barrier so I had to climb above the crowd. Three important principles to remember when God promotions you.

First, Some stuff that looks like promotion is correction. "Zacchaeus said look Lord, I give half of my goods to the poor and if I have taken anything from anyone by false accusation I will restore fourfold."

Because God has promoted me now I have to work on my private
Stuff so my public stuff will be correct. "Jesus was going to pass that way." Jesus wanted to come to Zacchaeus' house, but first Zacchaeus had to admit what he had did wrong before he promoted.

Secondly, God will use anything to get you in order. When he
climbs up Jesus noticed him. Jesus looks up, but Zacchaeus must come down. We spend countless hours trying to put ourselves up on that platform of success.

Jesus is the only one who can promote you. Psalm 75:6-7 "For promotion comes neither from the east nor the west nor from the south, but God is the judge. He puts one down and exalts another". You may be up in the world, but you got to come down so the Lord can deal with you. "Zacchaeus make haste and come down."

Thirdly, If you want God to stay at your house, you have to elevate your thinking. When Zacchaeus came down. Jesus spoke to him, "today I must stay at your house. "Eye has not seen, ear has not heard, nor has entered into the heart of man the things that God has prepared for them who loved Him, but God has revealed unto them that love Him." 1 Corinthians 2:9.

You have to think differently, you have to think bigger if you want God to stay at your house. You have got to think above the crowd. You can't let the crowd control your thinking. You have got to elevate your thinking and your praise so that God can come down and live with you.

CHAPTER TEN

IT'S ALL ABOUT THE KING

LUKE 19:31-40

31 If any man ask you, why do ye loose him? thus shall ye say unto him, Because the Lord hath need of him.

32 And they that were sent went their way, and found even as he said unto them.

33 And as they were loosing the colt, its owners said unto them, Why loose ye the colt?

34 And they said, The Lord hath need of them.

35 And they brought him to Jesus; and they cast their garments upon the colt, and they set Jesus on it.

36 And as he went, they spread their clothes in the way.

37 And when he was come near, even at the descent of the Mount of Olives, the whole multitude of the disciples began to rejoice and praise God with a loud voice for all the mighty works that they had seen,

38 Saying, Blessed be the King who cometh in the name of the Lord; peace in heaven, and glory in the highest.

39 And some of the Pharisees from among the multitude said unto him, Master, rebuke thy disciples.

40 And he answered, and said unto them, I tell you that, if these should hold their peace, the stones would immediately cry out.

Palm Sunday is about being ready when He comes.

The people of Jerusalem were celebrating Jesus because

was the sacrificial lamb to take away the sin of the world. He made it possible for us to reconnect with the Father through the shedding of His blood. Palm Sunday is a celebration in his honor. Jesus rode into Jerusalem and a party broke out. Everybody ought to praise God. When you praise God your praise gets God's attention. Some did not know what it was about. It's about if you stand for God; He will stand for you. It's about if you want more blessings you've gotta give more praises. God has been too good to you for you not to praise Him. Even when you facing a period of contradiction you still got to expect celebration.

We see in verse 31, Place and responsibility. If you want Jesus to come where you are you've gotta praise Him where you are. Your praise is important to God. "If any man ask you, Why do ye loose him? Thus shall ye say unto him, Because the Lord hath need of him." If anybody ask you why you are getting your praise on tell him or her it's important to God that I get my praise on. God has given me a cause to celebrate. The Blood of Jesus has cleansed me.

Your praise is important to God because it shows your responsibility to glorify God. Praise releases the power of God to do miraculous things. Jesus gave his disciple an assignment "to loose a colt." The Word tells us "let everything that has breath praise the Lord," some of us can't praise Him because we are tied down. Some of us tied to tradition tied to our feelings, and some are tied to the opinion of what others might think of us if we get my praise on.

What is praise? Praise is the means by which we express our joy to the Lord. Paul said, "let us offer the sacrifice of praise to God continually, that is, the fruit of our lips, giving thanks to his name," (Hebrews 13:15). Sometimes I don't feel like praising the Lord, I have to force my way through. That's why it's call sacrifice! When praises go up blessings come down. It does not matter what contradictions you are dealing with if you get your praise on.

God will eliminate your problems through your praise. When King Jehoshaphat had a problem, he began to praise God and God released His awesome power to destroy the enemy. When Paul and Salis were in jail they got their praise on and the doors flew open. If you want to see a turn around you've gotta get your praise on.

We see in verse 37, the power of recall. When I think about the goodness of Jesus and all that he has done for me my soul cries hallelujah.

" And when he was come nigh, even now at the descent of the Mount of Olives, the whole multitude of the disciples began to rejoice and praise God with a loud voice for all the mighty works that they had seen." (Isaiah 53: 4-10.) 10 " Yet it pleased the Lord to bruise him; he hath put him to grief: when thou shalt make his soul an offering for sin he shall see his seed, he shall prolong his days, and the pleasure of the Lord shall prosper in his hand."

When I recall the *punishment* that Jesus took for me it adds power to my testimony. "And they overcame him by the blood of the Lamb, and by the word of their testimony." Revelation 12:11. "Without the shedding of blood is no remission." Hebrews 9:22. The reason why some people don't have any power is they have lost the ability to recall what Jesus has done for them. See John 3:16 "God so loved the world He gave His only begotten son…" There is always something to praise God for. When I think about the goodness of Jesus and all that He did for me my soul cries hallelujah.

There are so many unfortunate things happening. Somebody just had an accident, somebody just died, or somebody just had a heart attack. When these bad things haven't happen to you; you have something to praise God for. "And when he came nigh" When He shows up He will turn things around. It does not matter what you are going through, Jesus will help you get through it. Watch this, everybody got his or her praise on. "The whole multitude of the disciples began to rejoice and praise God with a loud voice for all the mighty works that they had seen."

In verse 40 we see, proof and readiness. There are three ways to prove that you are ready to experience explosive prosperity. (1) Receive Jesus as the proof that

God loves you. See John 3:16 When He got ready to save us, He gave Jesus as the sacrificial offering for our sins. The disciples were listening to the Pharisee trying to talk them out of their praise. The Bible says, "If these should hold their peace, the stones would immediately cry out."

I am ready to represent. I'm not going to go with the crowd and sit on my praise. (2) My firstfruit is proof that I love Him giving him my best. He gave His best, and I'll represent through my giving best. See 26: 10. "And now, behold, I have brought the firstfruits of the land, which thou O Lord, has given me. And thou shalt set it before the Lord thy God, and *worship* before the Lord thy God." I'll represent in worship when I give the firstfruit.

When you represent with the firstfruit you will prosper with explosive prosperity. See Proverbs 3:9-10. Firstfruit equals your barns being filled with plenty and your *presses bursting* out with new wine. (3) Your firstfruit is proof that you are ready to prosper. God will give you *explosive prosperity*. Your obedience to worship with the firstfruit entitles you to the promises. Your faith causes you to possess the promises. Your Prosperity comes when you release the first fruit. The firstfruit obligates God to bless you. I am determined to receive what God has for me. I can't allow the devil to chump me down by not giving the firstfruit. The firstfruit is holy. It belongs to God.

Satan is trying to get you to disobey God. "And some of the Pharisees from among the multitude said unto him, Master, rebuke thy disciples." The Pharisees tried to stop the disciples from giving up the praise that was due to the Lord, but Jesus "answered and said unto them, I tell you that, if these should hold their peace, the stones would immediately cry out." The Pharisees were "hating on" the disciples because they got their praise on. The devil will hate on you when you worship with the firstfruit and get your praise on.

If you are ready to represent, God is ready to bless you. If you stand up for God He will stand up for you. God has been too good too you for you not to represent. It's all About the King!

CHAPTER ELEVEN
THE JOSHUA GENERATION

JOSHUA 1:1-3

1 Now after the death of Moses, the servant of the Lord, it came to pass that the Lord spoke unto Joshua, the son of Nun, Moses' minister, saying

2 Moses, my servant, is dead; now therefore arise, go over this Jordan, thou and all this people, unto the land, which I do give to them, even to the children of Israel.

3 Every place that the sole of your foot shall tread upon, that have I given unto you, as I said unto Moses.

It's time for you to get excited about your future. God has great things in store for you. Supernaturally, He is turning things around in your favor. You are the Joshua generation. You have been chosen by God to demonstrate the kingdom of God in the earth. God relates to persons through covenant. He has selected you to receive the mantle of those who will deliver what they advertise. The mantle is the symbol of authority. God has given you the authority to represent Him in the earth. You are the ones who will possess the promises of God. You are behind schedule but its not too late to walk into your destiny and to experience the blessings of God! You are the Joshua generation.

What is a Generation? A generation is a period of time between the birth of parents and the birth of their children; all of the people alive during that time. Generation comes from the word "genus" means race, or kind. What you put into your life is what you will get out of your life. Your faith will give birth to what you believe. Faith is the substance of things hoped for. What kind of substance does your faith generate? The faith you have will manifest itself in the life of your children. God is a God of generation. " I will continue this everlasting covenant between me and your offspring forever. And I will always be your God and the God of your descendants after you." For example, Abraham, Isaac, and Jacob represent a generation. The Old Testament uses generation as a measure of time. Although a generation sometimes covers up to a hundred years the normal generation is forty years.

We see in *verse 1,* promise and possession. God has given you a promise it is up to you to take possession of it. "Now after the death of Moses the servant of the Lord it came to pass, that the Lord spake unto Joshua the son of Nun, Moses' minister, saying."

If you want the promises of God to come true in your life, you've gotta believe so you can receive. You must be energetic about the things the God has promised you. When you boldly agree with God you will see the promises come truth in your life. Now is the time to believe God.   You are the Joshua generation. You've gotta start talking like it. You've gotta start living like it. And you've gotta start acting like it's so even before you see it. What you confess in the natural is taking place in the spiritual. You've gotta start declaring your destiny. Eventually you will see what you have been declaring. It's the time for the Joshua to rise up and walk in destiny. The Bible says, that Abraham…"calleth those things which be not as though they were, He staggered not at the promise of God though unbelief; but was strong in faith, giving glory to God." Romans 4:17,20.

We see in *verse 2,* your past is in competition with your future. Don't allow the things of your past to rob you of the things of your future. You have an incredible future, but you must not allow your past to interfere. "Moses my servant is dead; now therefore arise, go over this Jordan, thou, and all this people, unto the land which I do give to them, even to the children of Israel."

"Moses is dead." There were some that could not go forward with Joshua because they were looking back at Moses. God was calling for His people to move on, they were stuck in the past. Stop focusing on your yesterday start focusing on your future. Now is the time to capture your season. People who have been hurt in a relationship and refuse to get involve with somebody else are stuck in past. Now is the time to get into the flow of God. God is telling you how you can enjoy the promise of today. Get with what God is doing and don't allow the things of your past to rob you of the things of your future.

Change is difficult when you have become comfortable during a thing a certain way. We all have a natural resistance to change; however, we are all recipients of change. Had not God moved us from where we were in life, we would not be who we are today. The death of Moses brought change. Joshua was a type of Christ. His leadership was going to take them to another dimension. He was ready to lead, but they were not ready for change. If they had accepted his leadership they would have enjoyed extraordinary victory.

Joshua name means (Jehovah-Savior). Joshua was a type of Christ. They would have been siting in a high, wealthy and exalted place…a place where relationship is going on. This tells us that for the miracle of change to take place it is important to be rooted in a spiritual place, i.e., Christ. In other words, we must be in the right place for the right thing to happen. God had given His people an invitation through covenant, to enjoy His promised presence, but they refused to change. Their past was a barrier to possessing their future.

In *verse 3,* we see deputized and destiny. You have been deputized by God to walk into your destiny. V.3 "Every place that the sole of your foot shall tread upon, that have I given unto you, as I said unto Moses."

You have been deputized by God to own the land. "But as many as received him, to them gave he power to become the sons of God, even to them that believe on His name." John 1:12. You need God's power in your life to subdue what God has given you permission to have. You can't take authority in the flesh, but you can win it in the spirit*!*

This is your season, to win it. "Now faith is the substance of things hoped for, and the evidence of things not seen." Hebrews 11:1. Now is the time to walk into it. You have access to go to the next level. You have power, Greek Dumas, dynamite – explosive power. "Now unto Him that is able to do exceeding abundantly above all that we can ask or think according to the power that works in us." Ephesians 3:20.

Your victory is on the inside of you. I would like to close with one of my favorite cartoon television series, Batman. I like Batman because he is the capped crusader fighting crime in Gothem City. Batman never walked from a battle he away stood up to every challenge and was victorious. He knew what his mission was. Batman won every battle because it was written in the script. Well its been written in the script for us that we win. Our mission is to possess the promises of God. We are the Joshua generation the ones who will possess the promises of God. We have been deputized by God to walk into our destiny. We have power to win it. Victory is ours because "greater is He that is in us than he than is in the world." 1 John 4:4.

You gotta start declaring your destiny. Now is your season to win it. You the head, and not tail, above and not beneath you are the lender and not the borrower. You gotta believe that you can do what the word says you can do.

You can be who the word says you can be. You can have what the word says you can have.

CHAPTER ELEVEN
IT'S TIME TO BOUNCE BACK

EPHESIANS 6:10-13

10 Finally, my brethren, be strong in the Lord, and in the power of his might.

11 Put on the whole armour of God, that ye may be able to stand against the wiles of the devil.

12 For we wrestle not against flesh and blood but against principalities, against powers, against the rulers of the darkness of this world, against spiritual wickedness in high places.

13 Wherefore take unto you the whole armour of God, that ye may be able to withstand in the evil day, and having done all, to stand.

Paul wrote to the church at Ephesus exposing the evils of the day. Although Ephesus stood as the pillar within the Christian community, Paul cautioned them not to comprise with culture.   Satan is scheming against you. Paul wanted them to learn how to extinguish the flaming arrows of Satan.

The Romans called her Diana, the Greeks called him Artichmus; Paul called them the *"schemes of the devil."* Ephesus was the leading city in Asia thus the Greek/ Roman influence had tiptoed into the church. Magic and idol worship had become the order of the day.   The influence of Diana was real; it extended beyond the religious culture into the banking world.

Paul encouraged the church that God would take care of them. Although, the goddess Diana represented a lifestyle of economic stability God had promised He would take care of His people.   Paul encouraged them to be strong in

Christ and not in culture. The Christians at Ephesus experience tremendous hardship. When devastation threatens their financial stability God gave the prescription to – Bounce Back with Jesus!

It's time to be Strong in the Lord. We see in *verse 10* that God has made it possible for us to oppose the devil. Finally, my brethren, be strong in the Lord, and in the power of His might."

God has deputized you stand against the attacks of the devil. Power (Gk.) Dumas – dynamite: God gave you dynamite potential. He has given you the power to take action. Faith plus action equals substance. Remember "Faith is the substance of things hoped, and the evidence of things not seen," (Hebrews 11:1).

Deuteronomy declares that our covenant with God covers us economically. "Remember the Lord your God who gives you the power to get wealth, that He may establish His covenant with you." (Deuteronomy 8:18) Be strong in the Lord he will cover you financially.   There is no need to default with the devil, be strong in the Lord. The devil will tempt you, but you must be strong in the Lord. Understanding is a great thing.

It's time to understand the kind of war we are fighting. The War

that we are involved is filled with wickedness. We see in *verse 12* we must know the enemy. But remember, "in all your getting get understanding," understand this: The Battle is Not Yours but God's.

"For we wrestle not against flesh and blood, but against principalities, against powers, against the rulers of the darkness of this world, against spiritual wickedness in high places."

In order to win a war, you need a battle plan. Let God fight your battles. If you try to fight this battle by yourself you will loose. You cannot fight the devil with eight track ideas in a CD world. This battle is spiritual...

America is at war with the wrong enemy. Osama bin Laden is not the real enemy, Satan is. If we kill bin Laden, then the spirit of bin Laden will live. "The battle is not against flesh and blood, but against principalities..." The battle is spiritual!

The movie Harry Potter is a spirit battle. The movie like the goddess Diana is shrouded with demonic influences. It is based upon a boy who attends a school of wizards. There is another similarity – money. The movie showed in 9,000 theaters in a single day.   Some schools have arranged field trips for students to see this movie. Do the math, bad company corrupt good morals. Parents, it's time that we bounce back with the word. Watch this, get your Bibles: "When thou art come into the land which the Lord thy God giveth thee, thou shalt not learn to do after the abominations of those nations.

There shall not be found among you anyone who maketh his son or daughter pass through the fire, or who useth divination, or an observer of times, or an enchanter, or a witch, Or a charmer, or a consulted of mediums, or a wizard, or call forth the spirits of the dead," (Deuteronomy 18: 9-11). The enemy is bully!

It's time to recognize that the devil does not play Fair. In *verse 13* we see

had to believer to open their eyes to recognize. Recognize comes from the Latin word *"recognitio."* It is a compound word. When we break down the compound word recognize [re] plus [cognize] *re* means back, and *cognize*, which means to know, or understand. When you come under attack, you recall the last attack and understand that he is up to the same old tricks.

It is believed that Paul had the Roman solider in view when he wrote this letter to the Church at Ephesus. This figure of the Christian as a warrior impressed Paul to write encouraging them to stand. The key to your survival is to take a "position."

Your position is what you believe is right. Sometimes the devil tries to bully you, leading you into doing the wrong thing. You must remember that you are a <u>"person of purpose!"</u> You must not let him lead you. You must let him know that you gotta bounce!

Remember because you are a person of purpose: "use every piece of God's armor to resist the enemy in the time of evil, so that after the battle you will still be standing firm." (New Living Translation)

Put On:

- Belt of Truth

- Breastplate of Righteousness

- Shoes of the gospel

- Shield of faith

- Helmet of Salvation

- Sword of the Spirit/Word of God

- Praying Always

Remember that your strength is in the Lord, in the power of His might.

A. When sickness comes, let sickness know *"By Jesus stripes I am healed." (Isaiah 53:5)*

B. When trouble comes, let trouble know *"God is a present help in the time of trouble."(Psalms 46:1)*

C. When confusion comes, let confusion know *"God will keep me in perfect peace whose mind is stayed upon Him." (Isaiah 26:3)*

You were created to rule with Christ. You were created to win. You were created to be the head and not the tail. God gave the formula to defeat the devil. JESUS!

CHAPTER TWELVE
AND INCREDIBLE WITNESS

ACTS 1:3

3 To whom also He showed himself alive after his passion by many infallible proofs, being seen of them forty days, and speaking of the things pertaining to the kingdom of God.

Jesus was an incredible witness because he had passion. He suffered in the garden and on the cross. Passion is suffering. When you understand that suffering is a part of the process in developing you, you won't fight the process. It doesn't matter what it looks, you are on your way to becoming an incredible witness.

What does the word incredible means? Incredible means extraordinary. You won't mine "Weeping" because you know that it's only for a season. When the season is over you will be an extraordinary witness for Jesus.

It doesn't matter what I'm going through now, God has promised to bring me "joy in the morning." God has destined you to do great things for Him. You need power to do what God has called you to do. Power follows Passion.

When you have passion God will make you an incredible witness for Him. People are looking for extraordinary results of the kingdom. We must be able to deliver what we advertise. You are God's agent to make good on His promise: "bring the good news to the poor, to heal the broken hearted, to preach deliverance to the captives, and the recovering of sight to the blind."

Jesus got rid of the grave clothes. He showed His power after the tomb. Some of our situations have been wrapped in grave clothes. We are living our lives in contradiction of the covenant promises. We've got to get out of our grave clothes just Like Jesus did. We've got to get up! We can't lay in the grave and die. We've got to rise above our situation; we've got rise above our contradictions. After His passion, He showed His power. We've got to walk in power. Walk in the power of the word and the kingdom promises. Wherever there is someone who shows passion, God's power will be there.

We see in *1 Kings 17:13; 18:42,* anointing and miracles. God's power was with Elijah because he guarded the anointing. What is the anointing? The anointing is the presence of God working in your life. When you life have results it is because of the anointing. There is only explanation that could explain a miracle in your life. God did it. That's what happen for the widow of Zarephath. Elijah was an incredible witness because he cherished the anointing on his life. Can God trust you with the anointing? If you cherish the anointing on your life you will become an incredible witness for God too. God will use you to perform a miracle from a mess. Power follows passion.

We see in *Mark 5:25-30,* faith and substance. When you have faith, there will be substance. The woman with an incredible problem needed an incredible cure. She had an issue of blood for twelve years. She was determined to see Jesus so she could get some help. She was determined to stop living with minuses. She became an incredible witness.

Logic said there was no use to try, but she was determined. Logic said you have lost too much blood. Logic said there are too many people waiting to see Jesus. She was determined and pressed pass her logic to see Jesus.

Research said that Jesus was never going to pass through that city again. If she would have listen to logic she would have miss opportunity to become an incredible witness of what God can do. Jesus said, "who touched me."

The bible says "virtue life Him." Virtue means power left Him. Her passion made a withdrawal of His power to be healed. That's incredible! Power follows passion. God wants you to make a withdrawal. Your faith is your access to make a withdrawal for your relationship, your friendship, and your stewardship. "Without faith we cannot please God."

With passion, she broke through to another dimension. She was the first to receive healing from touching His clothes. Afterwards, the Bible says that multitudes sought to touch His clothes because a woman of passion moved in faith. She became an extraordinary witness because she pushed passed logic and got her healing. When you push pass your logic you will get your breakthrough. Power follows passion.

Faith will move mountains, but fear creates a mountain. We need a passion for Jesus. We must learn to live through the see nothing days. This woman did not see anything for 12 years, but she still became an incredible witness. What kind of determination do you have? Are you willing to press pass your logic and become an incredible witness for the kingdom?

We see in *Matthew 14:17-18,* another miracle and multiplication. This is an incredible story. A little boy who had, two fish, and five loaves of bread becomes a feast, to feed five thousands. That's incredible! When you get down to nothing, God is up to something. God is getting ready to bring multiplication to you if can trust Him with what you have. Wherever He finds passion, He releases His incredible power to do the miraculous.

Jesus had passion to serve the people. Five thousand people in a desert with no food. The disciples said we are down to nothing, but what they did not know that Jesus was up to something. He said, "bring them here to me."

You don't have to worry when you put your situation in His hands. He has capable hands. He had trusted hands. When Jesus blessed and broke, and gave the loaves to his disciples and the disciples gave them to the multitude. And they did all eat, and were filled." That's incredible! When you give it to Jesus, He will give you an extraordinary blessing.

If you want incredible blessings…Give Him the tithe, He will open the
windows of heaven. When you give Him the firstfruits, He will give you explosive prosperity. That incredible! Your barns will be filled with plenty, and your presses shall burst out with new wine.

There were twelve baskets full left. That's an <u>incredible</u> overflow. That's what God wants to do in your life. He wants to do the extraordinary thing in your life. He wants you to enjoy fullness and overflow! If you want to reach your incredible overflow, and become an incredible witness for the kingdom you've gotta stay in step with God.

Seasons are important. We are in an incredible season of overflow.

CHAPTER THRITEEN
ON YOUR MARK GET SET GO
EPHESHIANS 4:20-23

20 But ye have not so learned Christ,

21 If so be that ye have heard him, and have been taught by him, as the truth is in Jesus:

22 That ye put off concerning the former manner of life the old man, which is corrupt according to the deceitful lusts,

23 and be renewed in the spirit of your mind.

There are many exciting things that you can take advantage of if you are prepared; however, if you are not prepared they will pass you by. The year of overflow is here. It's a new opportunity for you to come alive in 2005. You can experience renewal when you are on your mark, when you get set, and when you have made the decision to go the distance…" You can only run the race, if and when, you set aside anything or anyone that is hindering you from putting forth your best effort.

Every race has a referee. They assign you a lane and ask you to get set. And when, all your hard work to prepare for this race is about to be judged… the gun is shot and you're off!

The same applies, in our race for Jesus. You see, God is your referee. The word of God prepares you on your mark. You're set, when you've identified the call that he has placed upon your life. And now, It's time to go spread, teach and preach the gospel; bringing others to Christ…sharing what God has given and worked in you. The race has already begun. Are you ready? If you are, take your mark…

We see in verse 20, discipline and defeat. If you are discipline you can defeat your opponent. Each runner has an opponent to defeat. He/she must compete against others who are trained to win. Training takes discipline. Similarly, the Christian also has an opponent. He/she must compete to win against the temptations of the world.

"But ye have not so learned Christ; If so be that ye have heard him, and have been taught by him, as the truth is in Jesus:" I've said it before and I'll say it again. You don't have to come to church to know God. But, you do have to become a student of the word. When you become a student of the scriptures learn the true principles of leading a true Christian life.

Many are what I call spiritually deficient. You become spiritually deficient through a lack of discipline and a consistent prayer life.

ROMANS 12:1, 2

1 I beseech you therefore, brethren, by the mercies of God, that ye present your bodies a living sacrifice, holy, acceptable unto God, which is your reasonable service.

2 And be not conformed to this world, but be ye transformed by the renewing of your mind, that ye may prove what is that good, and acceptable, and perfect, will of God.

We see deliberate and destiny. You must be deliberate if your expect to reach your destiny. The race is won, even before the gun goes off. It's all in your mind-set. It is by our mind-set that you receive inspiration. It is by your mind-set that you experience defeat. If you believe that you can win, then you will do well. If you believe that you can't compete, why are you running the race? Your thoughts and beliefs determine your outcome.

"And be not conformed to this world; but be ye transformed by the renewing of the mind, that ye may prove what is that good, acceptable, and perfect will of God" Again, a choice has to be made. The way you choose to direct your thoughts determine the direction of your life. If we adhere to the scripture and let the Holy Spirit redirect and renew our minds, the Lord will do the rest. He shall direct our paths in the way that is pleasing to him, and not man.

I told you last week that you must not conform to world but be transformed into a new person. Well, it's more to it than that. If you do not believe that most behavior of the world is corrupting and selfish, then you have basically defeated the purpose of your transformation.

Let's be real. Although we have a new nature, we don't automatically think good thoughts or express the right attitudes. But if we continually yearn to be in the presence of God and express a desire to know God, we will be completely transformed in no time.

Think back to this time last year. Do you notice a change for the better? Do you notice a change in you spiritually? Although change is slow, we must acknowledge how far God has brought us and believe that he will take us even beyond all expectations.

HEBREWS 12:1, 2

1 Wherefore, seeing we also are compassed about with
so great a cloud of witnesses, let us lay aside every
weigh, and the sin
Which doth so easily beset us, and let us run with
patience
the race that is set before us.

2 Looking unto Jesus, the author and finisher of our
faith, who for the joy that was set before him endured

the cross, despising the shame, and is set sown at the right hand of the throne of God.

We see in verse one, decision and distance. You must make a decision if you want to go the distance. Once you determine, who you are in Christ Jesus, and make the effort to get to know him, you must make the decision to keep going…choose to do more…get the most for your service…try God.

The book of Hebrews talks about going the distance… Running the race for Jesus. You must be willing to take your mark… For, this is a race that requires endurance, persistence and a sustained effort.

"Let us strip off every weight that slows us down, especially the sin that easily hinders our progress."

Are you willing to give up whatever threatens your relationship with God? You know, the gambling, the Friday Night high, the all-nighters with E & J.

Are you willing to grow and become prosperous on his time schedule? Yeah, I know you want the BMW, that Cadillac Escalade…but you must ask God is it your time.

Are you willing to solve problems, man's way or God's way? It a time of trouble, who will chose to go to for answers? And if you choose God, will you be satisfied with his answer. Will you accept it or is this when we try and fix it our way. Sound familiar?

The devil preys on our weaknesses, looking for an opportunity to cause us to stumble. We must not take our eyes off Jesus. He must always be in sight.

CHAPTER FIFTHTEEN
MAN IN THE MIRROR
2 CORINTIANS 3:17-18

Everyday is a gift from God. You did not know yesterday when you were sitting up in third period that you would make to today. God has given you the ability to do great things. Psalm 68:19 "Blessed be the Lord, who daily loaded us with benefits." That means that everyday God gives you benefits. What are benefits? Benefits are things that help you. God helps you with stuff. Stuff like FCAT, volleyball, football, or the dance ministry, cheerleading or whatever you are doing.

How you spend your day show how you appreciate the day that God has given you. You need to be honest with yourself and take an honest look at yourself. You need a mirror to help you to be honest with yourself and call it like it is. Everybody needs a mirror. A mirror gives a reflection of who you are. If you want a true picture of yourself you need to look in a mirror.

You remember the wicked witch in Snow White. She asked

"Mirror, mirror on the wall; who's the fairest of them all?" The witch was obsessed with the desire to be the most beautiful woman in the land. She loved the mirror. She spoke to it with terms of endearment until one day the mirror gave her answer, and she didn't know which she hated more, Snow White or the mirror that refused to lie. Mirrors don't lie. Mirrors will tell you the truth. Everyday you lie to yourself is another you spend in bondage. You've gotta get real with the man in the mirror. God wants you to take a contemplated look at the man in the mirror.

We see importance and mirror. Why is it important to look in a mirror? Mirrors will tell you the truth. A mirror reveals what it sees. The Holy Spirit is a mirror that reveals your true identity in Christ. "Now the Lord is that Spirit: and where the Spirit of the Lord is, there is liberty." It is important to flow with the Spirit. God wants you to be a pattern of Christ and not a paradox of

Christ. You need the Spirit to help you enjoy your freedom in Christ. "Stand fast therefore in the liberty wherewith Christ hath made us free, and be not entangled again with the yoke of bondage." Galatians 5:1.

You need a mirror to help you see stuff that is out of place. For example, your shirt may be hanging out and you don't know it until you get in the mirror. OR, your make up may have rubbed off and you don't know it until you get in the mirror. The mirror helps you get things in place. Shakespeare said it best "to thine own self be true." If you are going to be true with yourself you've gotta tell it like it is. Don't stop looking in the mirror. God is going to use you to impact the world for Christ...

We see truth and mirror. The mirror will open your eyes to the truth. "But we all, with open face beholding as in a glass the glory of the Lord." The Holy Spirit is a mirror. He's a mirror to help us with our spiritual stuff that is out of place. The Holy Spirit works like an apartment manager. Every month you pay rent but you don't own it. If there is Stuff in your apartment that is against regulation the apartment manager tells you to get it out. That's what the Holy Spirit does He reminds you of stuff that should not be in your life and tells you to get rid of it. "What? Know ye not that your body is the temple of the Holy Ghost which is in you, which ye have of God, and ye are not your own? For you are bought with a price: therefore glorify God in your body, and in your spirit, which are God's." 1 Corinthians 6:19-20.

He reminds us that we don't belong to ourselves. The Holy Spirit opens your eyes and reveals your true identity. Paul's prayer for the Church at Ephesus was that "The eyes of your understanding being enlightened; that ye may know what the hope of his calling is, and what the riches of the glory of his inheritance in the saints." Ephesians 1:18. God is concerned about your private life that's why He gave you the Holy Spirit as an apartment manager to open our eyes. What's in your private life will show up in your public world.

We see mirror and reflection. God wants the man in the mirror to be a reflection of His glory. What is glory?

Glory Hebrew means *"weight", or "importance".* Why are men struggling to become something they already are? "Changed into the same image from glory to glory, even as by the Spirit of the Lord." We were created in the image of God. Image in the Hebrew means "likeness."

We were created with the likeness of God. We where born with importance. If we were born with importance and significance we should go from "glory to glory." We should be going from one level of glory to next level of glory. Five reason men struggle to become something they already are:

1. <u>People</u> can hinder you from your purpose and destiny. You've gotta be with people who are walking in purpose. Your friends are your prophets of your future. You are known by the company you keep. "But the men that went up with him said, we are not able to go up against the people; for they are stronger than we." God is looking for people who will reflect who we are. Joshua and Caleb said we can "Let us go up at once, and possess it; for we are

well able to over come it." Numbers 13:30-31. God is not pleased with what we do but who we are...

2. <u>Powers</u> of darkness can hinder you from your purpose and destiny. "In whom the god of this world hath blinded the minds of them which believe not, lest the light of the glorious gospel of Christ, who is the image of God, should shine unto them." 2 Corinthians 4:4.

3. <u>Procrastination</u> can hinder you from your purpose and destiny. People are always talking about doing something in the future. I am going to start my diet next week. The only things that are going to happen are the things you schedule it to happen. "Beloved, now are we the sons of God, and it doth not yet appear what we shall be: but we know that, when he shall appear, we shall be like him; for we shall see him as he is." Now means needs over wants. People buy what they want and beg borrow and steal what they need. Discipline is delayed gratification.

4. <u>Memories of the past</u> can hinder you from your purpose and your destiny. There was a man out of his mind dwelling among the tombs. Greek word for tomb is *memory*. Memory is stuff that had happen in the past. The reason that we can't act consistently as the children of God. You can be delivered from something and when you see that person a memory take them back to who they were. You buckle at the knees and start sweating. It's impossible to be conscious of your God given consciousness and still sin. Mark. 5:3 "Who had his dwelling among the tombs; and no man could bind him, no, not with chains." If the devil can get you to forget who you are he can put you back in bondage. Memories can take you back to the past of the old man. You need a new vision. The clock is ticking. Your destiny is waiting.

5. <u>Prosperity</u> can hinder you from your purpose and your destiny. You don't need to wait on people to

give you permission to be successful. The anointing is the power to do "exceeding abundantly above all that you can ask or think according to the power that is in you." Ephesians 3:20. You must have understanding that God has already blessed you. Bless means to release hidden potential in you.

John Henry Faber did a study of prosessionary caterpillars they follow each in a circle. He placed a saucer full of pine needles two inches away. The caterpillars followed each other for six days. They just went around and around in circles. They died from starvation. They favorite food was two inches away. There are people just like that they will follow the crowd never do what they want to do. They just follow others, or the status quote. You got to make a decision now to do something. Romans say its height time to come The Holy Spirit always fall on the now. Our times are in His hands.

CHAPTER SIXTEEN
SET THE CRUSIE CONTROL
GALATIANS 6:9

9 And let us not be weary in well doing; for in due season
we shall reap, if we faint not.

When you have made the choice to go the distance
for Jesus. You must learn to pace yourself so you won't
become dissatisfied with your work. You need to learn
how to set the cruise control. A cruise control is a luxury

installed in some vehicles that allows you to determine your speed, cruising down the highway comfortably until you make to your destination.

Setting the cruise control in your life will keep you from growing frustrated and worn out. It allows you to go the distance. You've taken your mark, your course has been set and now…it's time to set your cruise control.

We see in verse 9, pace and speed. You must pace yourself if you expect to go the distance.

"And let us not grow weary." Busy Christians often get tired, but they should not become weary. Tired is merely a physical condition, but "weary" describes a spiritual attitude. We become weary, in part, from blaming God for our own sinfulness.

God sometimes uses our physical fatigue:

a) To cause you to look to him for satisfaction,

b) To possibly administer correction, as he forces your physical body to slow down; in order to be refueled,

c) To prepare you for a greater challenge.

Jeremiah 31:25 says, "for I have satisfied the weary soul, and I have replenished every sorrowful soul." This is god's promise. Physical fatigue may cause you t miss out on earthly fun and fellowship, but spiritual resources will enable you to grow stronger on the bed of affliction.

The term "let" is an act of willingness to hang on in there. It's a determination. *"Let"* is being tenacious about your commitment. It's an opportunity to reach your level of excellence.

Most jumbo jets upon take off; the pilot set their cruise control once they have reached an attitude of 35,000 feet. They know that is a safe level to avoid air pockets, and turbulence. The passengers can enjoy a good flight.

Watch this, if you want to reach excellence, you must set your attitude so you can cruise to your level of excellence. It has been said many times, your attitude determines your altitude.

Therefore, you must take on a renewed attitude to continue serving God; refueling the body and the soul. The body needs rest so you can stay on course so you can reach your destiny.

We see in second portion of verse 9, resume your good works. If you want to demonstrative good works you must give your body what it needs. I know that sounds like a non-spiritual expression. Rest is a part of our covenant promise. Once the body has been refueled through rest you can resume your good works.

What do you mean by resume? Resume means to pick up where you let off.   If you happen to have slowed down, resume your good works. Be tenacious, "While doing good." Are you doing good? Are you spreading the positive, or, are you doing nothing? Or, Are you missing in action.

Most live their lives like fans at a football game. They stand on the edge of the playing field, observing the contenders. They stand and cheer, boo and hiss. It never occurs, that they should be on the playing filed.

God did not bring you out of darkness into the marvelous light, in order for you to become a spectator but a contender. There is much work to be done. Christians should be encouraged to persevere.

What I'm trying to get you to see is the danger of being there and not knowing it. Some spend all their lives trying to get there and not know when they are actually in the place. Ask yourself. Do you want to be missing in action, or staying in action?

In the third portion of verse 9, we see cruising and the finish line. If you want to cruise pass the finish line you must not grow give up.

Keep it on cruise. Your ship will come in. "But in due season you shall reap if you do not lose heart." You must know your season. Due season is when what to expect has arrived. You have been there and done that… It is at this stage that you will reap the benefits for longevity.

It's payday!

Remember John Maxwell's timetable for success…

The wrong thing at the wrong time = disaster.
The right thing at the wrong time = resistance.
The wrong thing at the right time = mistake.
The right thing at the right time = Success!

This is where your blessings will occur. This is the harvest. Because you have stayed the course now you come into your season.

It's payday!

Action must be taken in your season. Watch this, what is a season? The word "season" is translated from the Hebrew word "zeman," which means an appointed time. It is fruit bearing time. If you miss your season, you'll miss your blessing…Don't let payday pass you by!

Your season is waiting on you its up to you to walk into it. It has been stated that "timing is everything". Understanding this makes for a great journey with God. For when we talk about our season we are really talking about timing. In Psalm 1:3, it stated that the one who operates within a responsible relationship with God will "prosper in due season." Your recognition that God's system of operating is governed by "due season" will go a long way in determining the extent of God's anointing in your life. Ecclesiastes 3:1 declares that "there is a time for everything and a season for every activity under the Heaven."

Paul, in his final years, teaches his son, Timothy, a vital lesson. It is not how well you start, but how you finish that matters most. Ultimately, it is how effectively we finish that leaves an indelible of lasting imprint in the sand of time.

Bishop Forten Sheen states: "He doesn't just teach him how to begin, for starting is not enough. He teaches him how to end." Ecclesiastes 7:8, (a) "the end of a thing is better than it's beginning."

Paul ends his life in a crescendo of wisdom and triumph. What a grand finale! When the book was closed and the coat was folded, the old man had maintained his integrity and retained his forte.

Paul knew his season. Paul showed up for payday…This message is simple. It doesn't matter how you start. It only matters how you finish. Success is achieved when the final tally comes in. What a testimony you'll finished the race.

CHAPTER SEVENTEEN

YOU ARE ON YOUR WAY THERE

PHILLIPPIANS 3:12-13

12 Not as though I had already attainted, either were already perfect; but O follow after for which also I am apprehended of Christ Jesus.

13 Brethren, I count not myself to have apprehended; but this one thing I do forgetting those things, which are behind, and reaching forth unto those things, which are before.

You are on your way there. There is a place called "there." It is not a neighborhood one lives in. You can't find it on a map. Neither money, nor education, nor influence can get you there. It is a place wise people seek. It is a place where your soul starts to sing the place that you sense with all that is in you: "This is where I am meant to be."

"There" is the place that God calls us to from the beginning, and most of us spend years, trying to make to get "there." So we run trying desperately to attain a place so difficult to articulate that most people do not understand what drives us. Like children playing tag, we get touched by this place called "there and then run and search, trying to find this place. We will get to the place called "there," if we allow God to lead us there.

You must know where you are. (V.12). "Not as thought I had already attained, either were already perfect." Paul knew where he was. He said that his goal was to know Christ, to be like Christ, and to be all Christ had in mind for him. Paul knew that he was not "there" yet. Do you know where you are? If you don't know where you are you could have gotten off the path to the place called "there." You must admit where you are and then confront what has brought you to this station in life. "Not as thought I had already attained, either were already perfect."

The word perfect means mature. Paul came to grip that he was immature about some things. He was now ready to correct those things. "When I was a child, I spoke as a child, I understood as a child, I thought as a child; but when I became a man, I put away childless things." It's time to grow up. It's time to put away your toys and pick up your tools.

Until you make an honest assessment of where you are you will never get "there." You will never reach maturity in handling matters of importance, financial or relational, until you confront where you are. Once you have made an assessment you can begin to compare "your "here" with your "there." Then you can embrace the desire within you that yearns to be where God wants you to be.

We see need to move. You must move from where you are so you can get to where you need to be. "But I follow after, if that I may apprehend that for which also I am apprehended of Christ Jesus." Your decision to move from where you are to where you need to be comes from a knowing that you were not created to be "here." You have a desire to be "there." Philippians 2:13. If you want to get there sometimes you must change your directions. Changing directions is as simple as "God said it; I believe it and that settle it." You must ask yourself what am I doing here when I suppose to be "there"? Elijah was not where he was supposed to be. Elijah the prophet was running from Jezebel. He went and hid in a cave. Elijah hid in the cave because of fear. God asked Elijah, "What are you doing here?" because He knew that he was not created to be "here" when he could be "there." 1 Kings 19:12-13. No one can confront your "here" but you. You must confront your fear.

When you discover your "here" is not your "there." There is no harm in not being "there" if you are on your way, if you are in hot pursuit of the place called "there." The real tragedy is when you're not even going in the right direction. It means you're lost and you haven't even begun the real journey. But the good news is that if you realize that you have been running in circles, you can stop and make today a starting place. Every journey must start somewhere, and the time is now.

Being in the right place is like a timing pattern in football. The quarterback gathers the players in a huddle so he can call the play. He tells the receiver, "go long I am going to throw you the ball." It's the receiver's job to be at the spot to catch the ball. If the receiver is there to catch the ball he can score a touch down. If you are where God wants you to be you will score a touch down for Jesus. Our journey for us to get to the place called "there" has to do with timing. It's important to be "there" so you can get to where you need to be. We must assess our present position if we are to move forward to "there."

You will get there if you fix your eyes on the path to getting "there." "Brethren, I count not myself to have apprehended; but this one thing I do, forgetting those things which are behind, and reaching forth unto those things which are behind." We will get to the place of spirit filled worship. We will get to the place of a beautiful sanctuary to call our own. We will get to the place where the Caleb's project will be finished, the building filled, and debt free. The only way we can maximize our moments is to make sure we are on the way to "there." The hard work, the fears, the obstacles, and challenges they will all become worthwhile because they are means to an end.

Cast off your past failures, mistakes, wrong turns, and dead-ends. Change your directions to make sure you are moving toward the calling that will allow you to find the deep soul satisfaction that comes from knowing that "there" is our destination. There is great joy in the journey in knowing you are moving in the direction that you were created for. Press on. You must forget the past and reach for your future. Don't let your past rob you of your future.

"Not as thought I had already attained, either were already perfect. But I follow after, if that I may apprehend that for which also I am apprehended of Christ Jesus. Brethren, I count not myself to have apprehended; but this one thing I do, forgetting those things which are behind, and reaching forth unto those things which are behind."

CHAPTER EIGHTEEN
DANCING IN THE DARK
MALACHI 3:10

10 Bring all the tithes into the storehouse, that there may be food in mine house, and test me now herewith, saith the Lord of hosts, if I will not open for you the windows of heaven, and pour out for you a blessing, that there shall not be room enough to receive it.

There are many things that separate believers from the world. One thing in particular is that we believe in covenant. A covenant is between two people. Covenant means that if you do this, then I will do that. What every believer has to come to understand is that God not only wants us to be saved, but He wants us to experience victory in our finances, but all of us will not experience victory if you are dancing in the dark. Dancing in the dark means that you are shouting, praising, and speaking in tongues but the windows in heaven are closed. The shades are draw and the curtains are shut. The windows in heaven are closed because you haven't been consistent with the Tithe. A lot of people who love the Lord are struggling in the area of finances because they are dancing in the dark.

We can see the physical lights all around us. But what I want to talk about today is not dancing in the physical light, but dancing without the heavenly light. When you want to sleep in on Saturday morning, the first thing you do is go close the window, pull down the shade and clothes the curtains tight. You are trying to make sure that absolutely no light gets in to disturb your sleep. When God has shut up the windows of heaven, absolutely no light can come in. When you rob God of His tithe, He cannot open up the windows of heaven. When we rob God of his tithe, we are dancing and praising God for what He's done, but we are dancing under a closed window. We are dancing in the dark.

We see in John 1:5, when there is darkness, there is no light. When there is no light, you can't see. When you can't see, you are liable to go in any direction. "The light shines through the darkness, the darkness can never extinguish it." When we have the light, we avoid walking blindly into the trap of the question "what should we give God?

Money tells where your heart is. You don't ever hear the crack addict complain about the price of crack going up, because he loves it. You don't hear beer drinkers and cigarette smokers complaining about the price of their habit. They love it; they don't care what it cost, so they spend their hard-earned money on it. If you say you love Jesus, then you don't mind giving your money to Him. If you don't you are robbing God. You are strong-arming Him. You are holding Him up and taking His money.

In verse 8 we see, the disinterested making a Sunday morning holdups. We don't want any Sunday morning "hold ups" at 4400 Power's Drive. " Will a man rob God?" WE have robberies on Sunday mornings. Do you know the difference between a burglar and a robber? A burglar will wait until you are gone, break into your stuff and be gone by the time you get back. A robber will stand up in your face, and say "Stick em up!" At offering time, you are saying, "Stick em up, God." A Sunday morning hold up!

How in the world can you rob the one who gave you water to drink, air to breath, a bed to sleep on, shelter over your head, healing for your body and deliverance? When you rob God, that means that everything you have is stolen because you bought it with stolen money. Simply because you didn't give the tenth to God.

We see in verse 10, your decision to bring all releases abundance and turn's the light on. The windows are open when you obey God. "Bring all the tithes into the storehouse so there will be enough food in my Temple." All not only means your tenth, but it means your offering too. The scripture doesn't say to bring your tithe after taxes. It says to bring all. If you pay Uncle Sam and tithe off of what's left, that is not all. All means all.

We see in (verse 10, b) God is ready to bring you into the next dimension with one blessing. A dimension is different from the next level. The next level is another step. Like 1,2,3,…But the number 10 is another dimension. God is ready to bring you into the next dimension. He is ready to give you one blessing can carry you for the rest of your life. One blessing can carry you for years. "If you do, says the Lord Almighty, I will open the windows of heaven for you. I will pour out a blessing so great you won't have enough room to take it in! Try it! Let me prove it to you! When you are ready to stop dancing in the dark and go to the next dimension. God will give you "a blessing" that will change your life forever. Your decision to bring the tithe will cause God to pour you out a blessing that will open the floodgates.

In First Kings 18:41-44, we see God is ready to open the floodgates. "Elijah said I hear a mighty rainstorm coming…Finally, the seventh time, his servant told him, I saw a little cloud about the size of a hand rising from the sea." God is going to hit this Church with an overflow of wealth. If you want to swim in the abundance you gotta stop dancing in the dark. *See Ezekiel 47: 1-5.*

CHAPTER NINETEEN
STAYING IN STEP WITH GOD
ACTS 13:22,36

22 And when he had removed him, he raised up unto them David to be their king; to whom also he gave testimony, and said, I have found David, the son of Jesse, am ma after mine own heart, who shall fulfill all my will.

You've gotta stay in step with God if you want to represent Him in the world. The greatest hindrance to the present move of God is the past move of God. The key to your success in ministry is to be sensitive to the spirit and to stay in step with God. If you want to be a part of the overflow, you've gotta follow closely with God so you won't miss your time of visitation. You can't afford to get out of step with Him and allow your blessings to slip through your fingers. What happens when you get out of step with God?

When your heart is not right you are out of step with God.

David was chosen to replace King Saul because he got out of step with God. "But God removed him from the kingship and replaced him with David." When you get out of step with God you will be removed and replaced. Jerusalem lost their visitation because they rejected Jesus. Jonah spent three nights in the belly of the whale because he did not want to preach to Nineveh. Samson lost his hair and his strength because he did not place any value of the call of God on his life. Esau lost his birthright because he did not see to need to fight for what was rightly his. When you try to redefine your purpose and get out of step with God you will lose.

Your heart has to be right in order to stay in step with God. "David was a man about whom God said, "David son Jesse is a man after my own heart, for he will do everything I want him to." Your heart is vitally important. The Bible teaches, "above all else, guard your heart, for it affects everything you do."

Coach Vince Limbordi of Green Bay Packer's; use to say when he would choose his players of the starting team. "It takes skill and muscle to play the game of football. He would rather have a player who had "heart" rather than skills and muscle. The one with the heart will play in the rain, cold, or snow because his heart was in it."

People who get out of step with God do so because their heart is not in it. When your heart is not in it shows. David's was in step with God because his heart was in it. Psalm 42:1 "As the deer panteth after the water brooks, so panteth my soul after thee, O God." Even when David got out of step with God he repented and got back in step. Psalm 51:1-2 "Have mercy upon me, O God, according to thy loving-kindness; according unto the multitude of thy tender mercies blot out my transgressions. Wash me thoroughly from mine iniquity, and cleanse me from my sin."

36 For David, after he had served his own generation by the will of God, fell asleep, and was laid unto his fathers, and saw corruption.

When you stay in step with God, He will open doors for you.

God opened a door for David to fight Goliath and win. David's father was given supernatural debt cancellation and he got a wife out of the deal. Because God opened the door for David, He will open the door for you. The key is staying in step with God. "Now this is not a reference to David, for after David had served his generation according to the will of God, he died and was buried, and his body decayed."

Staying in step with God doesn't mean that we are immortal, we will die, but we will leave a legacy. Our legacy will live on because we stayed in step with God. God set up a kingdom after David. David's generation was blessed because he stayed in step with God. When we stay in step with God, your generation will birth great men and women of God. Zech 12:8 "On that day the Lord will defend the people of Jerusalem; the weakest among them will be as mighty as King David! And the royal descendants will be like God, like the angel of the Lord who goes before them!" You might ask who are David's royal descendants? **Jesus.**

The Angel Gabriel confirmed God's agreement with David to Mary. You know the Christmas story: "You will become pregnant and have a son, and you are to name him Jesus. He will be very great and will be called the Son of the Most High. And the Lord God will give him the throne of his ancestor David. And he will reign over Israel forever; his Kingdom will never end! Mary asked the angel, "But how can I have a baby? I am a virgin." The angel replied, "The Holy Spirit will come upon you, and the power of the Most High will overshadow you. So the baby born to you will be holy, and he will be called the Son of God." Luke 1:31-35. "For a child is born to us, a son is given to us. And the government will rest on his shoulders.

These will be his royal titles: Wonderful Counselor, Mighty God, Everlasting Father, and Prince of Peace. His ever expanding, peaceful government will never end. He will rule forever with fairness and justice from the throne of his ancestor David. The passionate commitment of the Lord Almighty will guarantee this! Isaiah 9: 6-7. Because of David's character, God is going to establish a <u>millennium</u> kingdom on the order of righteousness and peace.

What does millennium kingdom means? Millennium means one thousand years of reigning with Christ. It will be a time of peace and prosperity, but it will also be problems for those who are not with Christ. It will a time of mercy, but there will also be misery. It will be a time that "the wolf and the lamb will eat together and the lion will eat straw like the ox, poisonous snakes will strike no more. In those days, no one will be hurt or destroyed on my holy mountain. I, the Lord, have spoken." Isaiah 66:12.

CHAPTER TWENTY

I SURVIVED

ACTS 14: 14-20

14 Which when the apostles, Barnabas and Paul, heard of, they tore their clothes, and ran in among the people, crying out,

15 And saying, Sirs, why do ye these things, We also are men of like passions with you, and preach unto you that ye should turn from these vanities unto the living God, who made heaven, and earth, and sea, and all things that are in them.

16 Who in times past allowed all nations to walk in their own ways.

17 Nevertheless, he left noting himself without witness, in that he did good, and gave us rain from heaven, and fruitful seasons, filling our hearts with food and gladness.

18 And with these sayings scarce restrained they the people, that they had not done sacrifice unto them.

You have too much going for you to quit now. God has given you the power to survive anything. He has given you the ability to overcome if you have the right prospective. Your prospective has a lot to do with your survival. The devil will do everything is his power to distract you from your ministry. It does not matter what you are going through you can endure it. If you can change how you look at your problem you can survive your problem. Your problem is a part of the process in developing you to be a survivor. You may not be able to change what you are looking at, but you can change how you look at it. You can't surrender to the devil when you are committed to reaching the world for Christ. Dogs don't bark at parked cars. If you aren't doing anything, you should not expect anything to challenge you. You are closer than you think. You are closer now than before. Where God is taking you, you've gotta have some boldness. When you have the courage to stand up to the devil, and let him know "I ain't going out like that." You will survive. Can we talk, let us talk? How can you say that you will survive?

When you have the right prospective you will survive. (V.14-15) "But when Baranabas and Paul heard what was happening, they tore their clothing in dismay and ran out among the people, shouting, Friends, why are you doing this? We are merely human being like yourselves! We have come to bring you the Good News that you should turn from these worthless things to the living God, who made heaven and earth, the sea, and everything in them."

Paul survived the slander of the Jewish men who poisoned the minds of the innocent bystanders because he had the right prospective about man who was healed. Your prospective has a lot to do with your survival. Have you notice that the church is always the first causality. V.19 "Now some Jews arrived from Antioch and Iconium and turned the crowds into a murderous mob." Anybody can persuade church people. Church people don't think for themselves therefore they give up at the first sign of trouble because they don't have the right prospective. When the pressure is on they don't think about giving up their jobs, they just give up church. They won't give up that frat brother or that sorority sister, they give up on God. I am here today proposing another position. Instcad of being persuaded by the enemy, change your prospective. Let the devil know I will survive this because of Jesus. The people who were once with Paul are now against him. It takes a strong trust in the Lord to survive when friends or so-called friends turn on you. You had to wrestle all night.

You had to start over, but you got your fight back. You got your joy back. You will start over again. You can survive anything when God is with you.

19 And there came there certain Jews from Antioch and Iconium, who persuaded the people, and having stoned Paul, drew him out of the city; and the next day he departed with Barnabas to Derbe.

Your problems are your preparation for something greater. "They stoned Paul, and dragged him out of the city, apparently dead. But as the believers stood around him, he got up and went back into the city. The next day he left with Baranabas for Derbe." The believers stood around Paul and prayed him back to health. Paul had a serious problem. The bible tells us that he was nearly dead. When you are nearly dead in you spiritual life, God can't use you and that's problem. The prayer of the believers gave Paul the power to overcome his problem. The problem that you overcome is preparing you for something greater. God pulled out the stops for Paul and He will pull out the stops for you because you were willing to go through what you went through. God will move whatever is in your way when you are willing to go all the way. God will use you to be an example for others to walk around the pitfalls of life. When the devil pushes you and you have the right perspective that's when God escorts you to the next level.

21 "After preaching the Good news in Derbe and making many disciples, Paul and Baranabas returned again to Lystra, Iconic, and
Antioch of Pisidia,

22 Where they strengthen the believers. They encouraged them to continue in the faith, reminding them that they must enter into the Kingdom of God through many tribulations."

God allowed them to push you into your blessing. They pushed Paul and Baranabas to the next level. They fired you, but you thank them for the push. The Jews pushed Paul to another place. They pushed him into his blessing. They pushed you into your blessing. Thank God for the push. Somebody listening to me, you have been pushed into your blessing. God allowed your enemies to push you into your blessing.

A friend was telling me about a conference where everybody was trying to get upstairs. There were so many crowding onto the elevator that the doors kept opening and closing that the elevator would not move. The elevator had reached its capacity of 4,000 lbs. It could not go up. Then some of the people realized that there were too many and they begun to get off. Then the elevator began to rise to the next level. Well New Generation, there were too many on our elevator who did not want to go to the next dimension so they got off so we could go up to the next dimension.

CONCLUSION

Supernaturally, God is getting ready to do so awesome things in your life. What was going to take ten years is going to happen in ten months. What was going to take ten months is going to happen in ten weeks. What was going to take ten weeks is going to happen in ten days. What was going to take ten days in going to happen in ten hours. What was going to take ten hours is going to happen in ten minutes. And what was going to take ten minutes is going to happen in ten seconds. Nothing can stop you He has given you the permission to go to the next dimension. What is permission? Permission is authority given by someone over you. God, the creator of the heaven and the earth has given you the permission to go to the next dimension. He is getting ready to make a supernatural turn around in your health, wealth, and in your wisdom.

He's going to blow your mind, but your attitude gotta be right. When God says that you are the head and not the tail, above and not beneath, blessed coming and going out…You've gotta believe it. Deut. 28. If you are ready for your increase you ought to praise Him like you know it's already done.

God is going to remove the limits off of your wealth, health and off of your wisdom so you can be a blessing to others. You can't do real ministry if you are bound. God is establishing generational wealth. Its time to get your stuff back.

There was a pastor who gave his son an all access pass to attend the Bayou classic but the son did not realize what he had. He had the opportunity to go and enjoy all of the events of the classic. He could have gone to the step show, the battle of the bands, even to the back stage concert to meet the special guest. He did not know what his father had given to him, and many of us don't know what our Father has given to us. He has given us the authority or the all access pass to go to the next dimension. When you go to the next dimension, you can hear from God in a more personal way. When you read God's word you will discover you have authority to make the unproductive productive. You can make an impartation into someone else's life. You can create jobs for the unemployed. You can provide housing for the homeless. God has given you the access to go to the next dimension. God is getting ready to blow your minds with what He is about to do, but gotta be free so you can set someone else free. It is my prayer that this book be a blessing to you as you go to the next dimension!